Tango

DAVID REMFRY

'O body swayed to music, O brightening glance.
How can we know the dancer from the dance?'

W. B. Yeats (1865–1939)

When at Hull College of Art, I became interested in imagery of people dancing. The subject provided a plausible way of drawing people in motion, of moving in an embrace. I had been to a few youth clubs and seen jive and various dance forms popular at that time. The best venue I found while at college was the Locarno Night Club, where I was able to make small drawings surreptitiously.

This was in effect the beginning of a love of dance and dancers. La Nacional and Triangulo were two of my favourite tango venues in New York City. The drawings in this book were made at Triangulo on 20th Street, where I was able to sit unnoticed.

Years earlier, before the two decades I spent living at the Hotel Chelsea in New York, I did go for tango lessons at Turnham Green in West London. While dancing with Heather, my patient instructor, I found it easy to imagine myself as an Argentinian. Of course, as soon as she left me to dance unguided, it all fell apart.

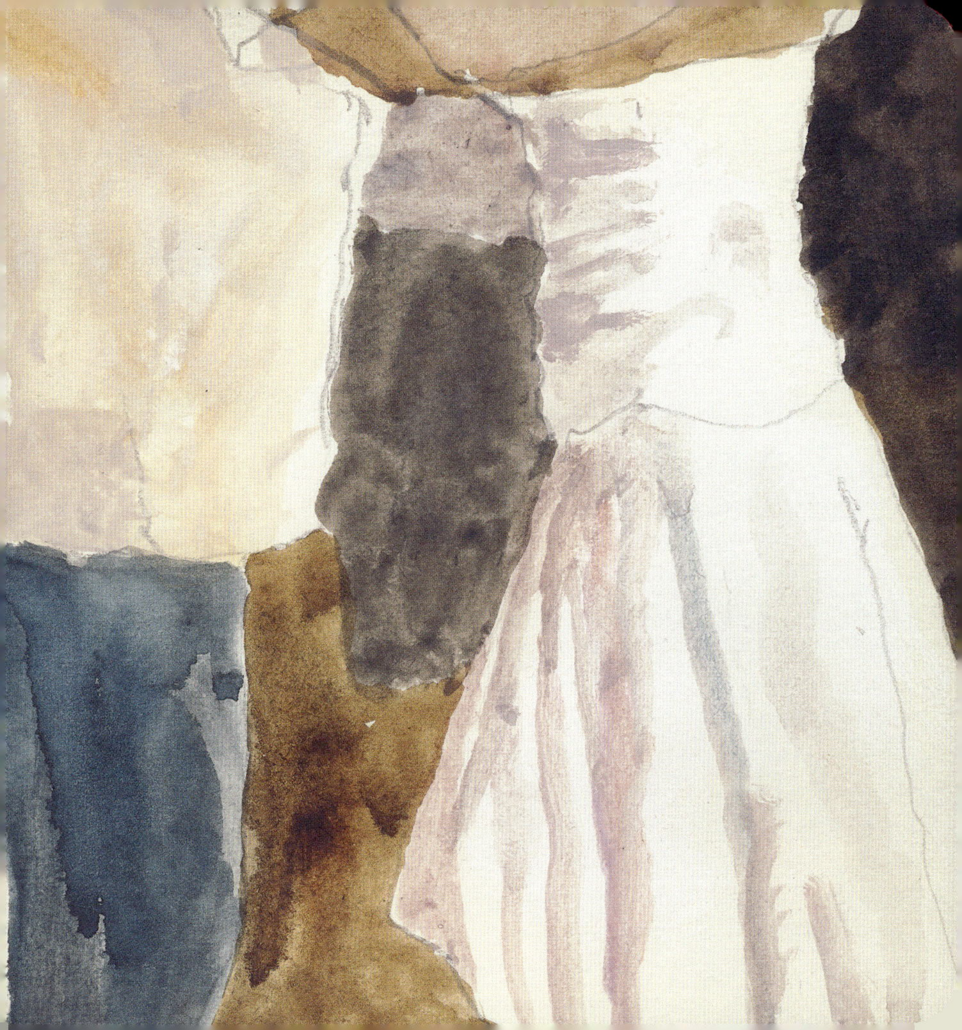

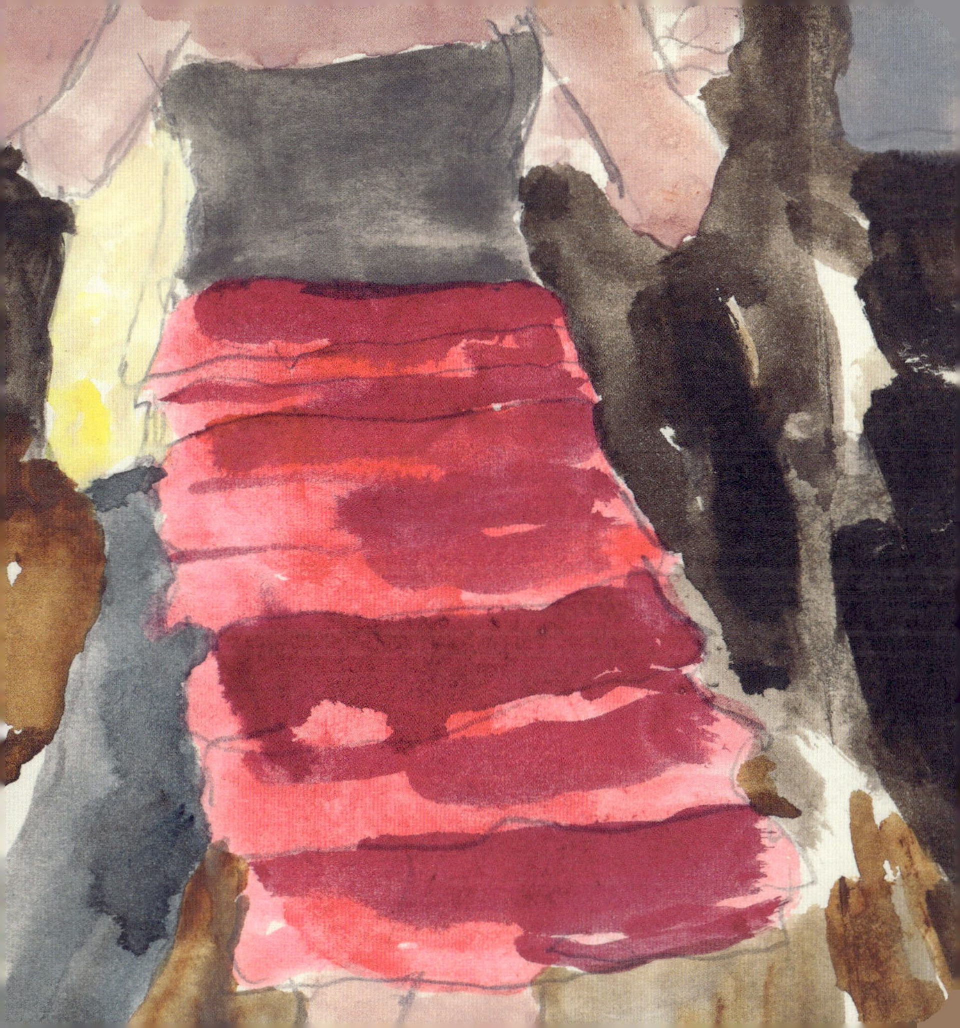

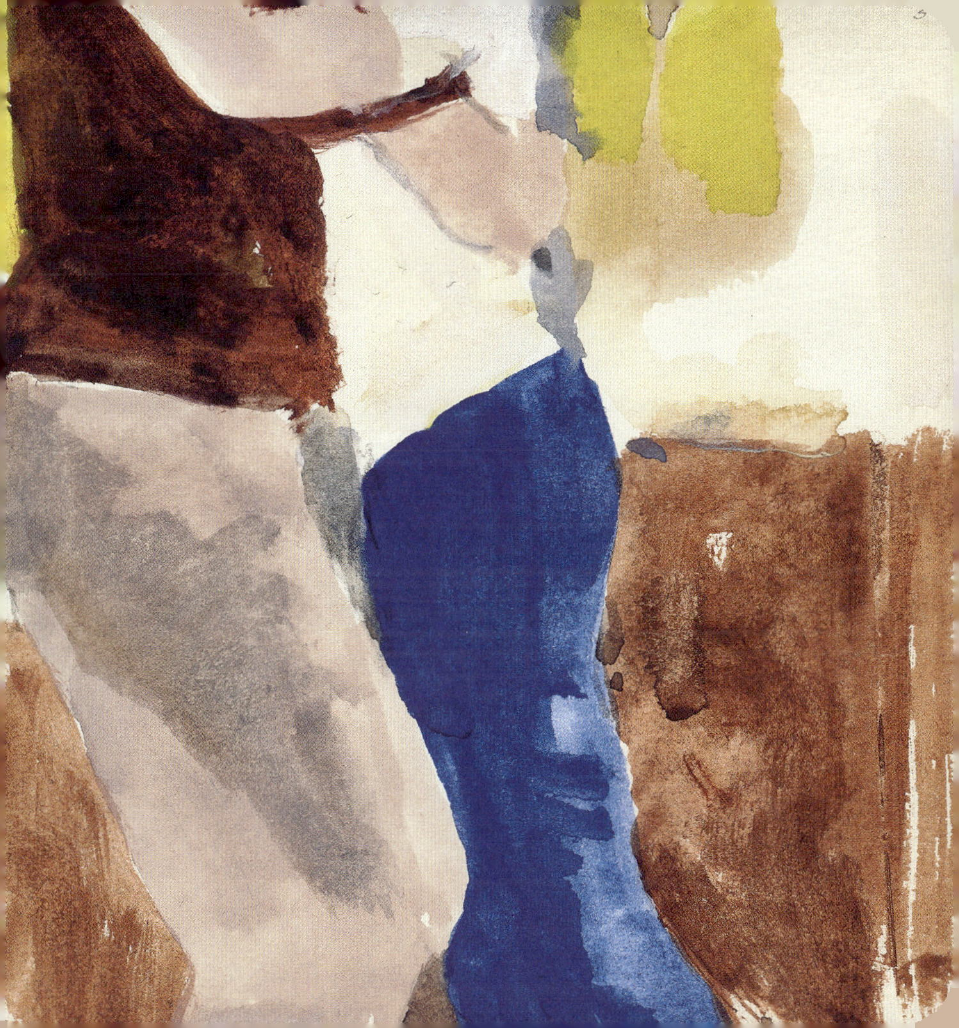

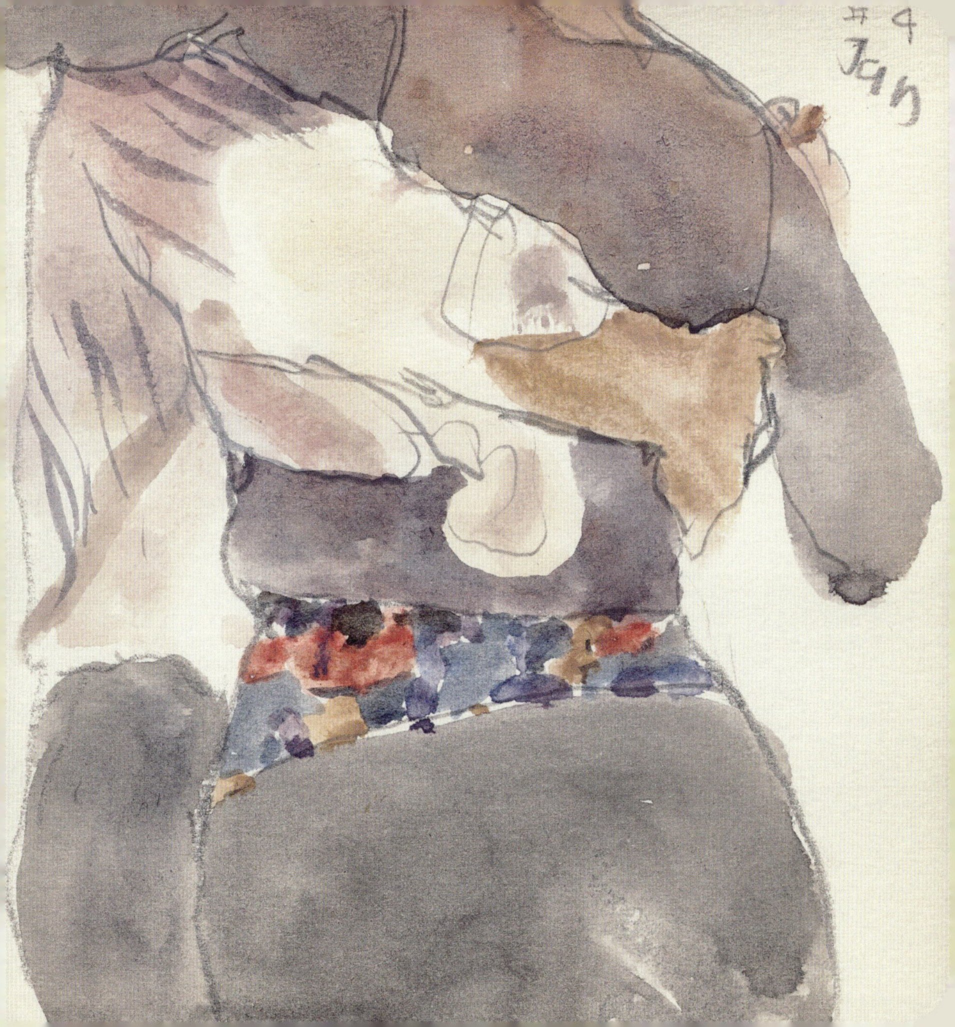
4 Jan

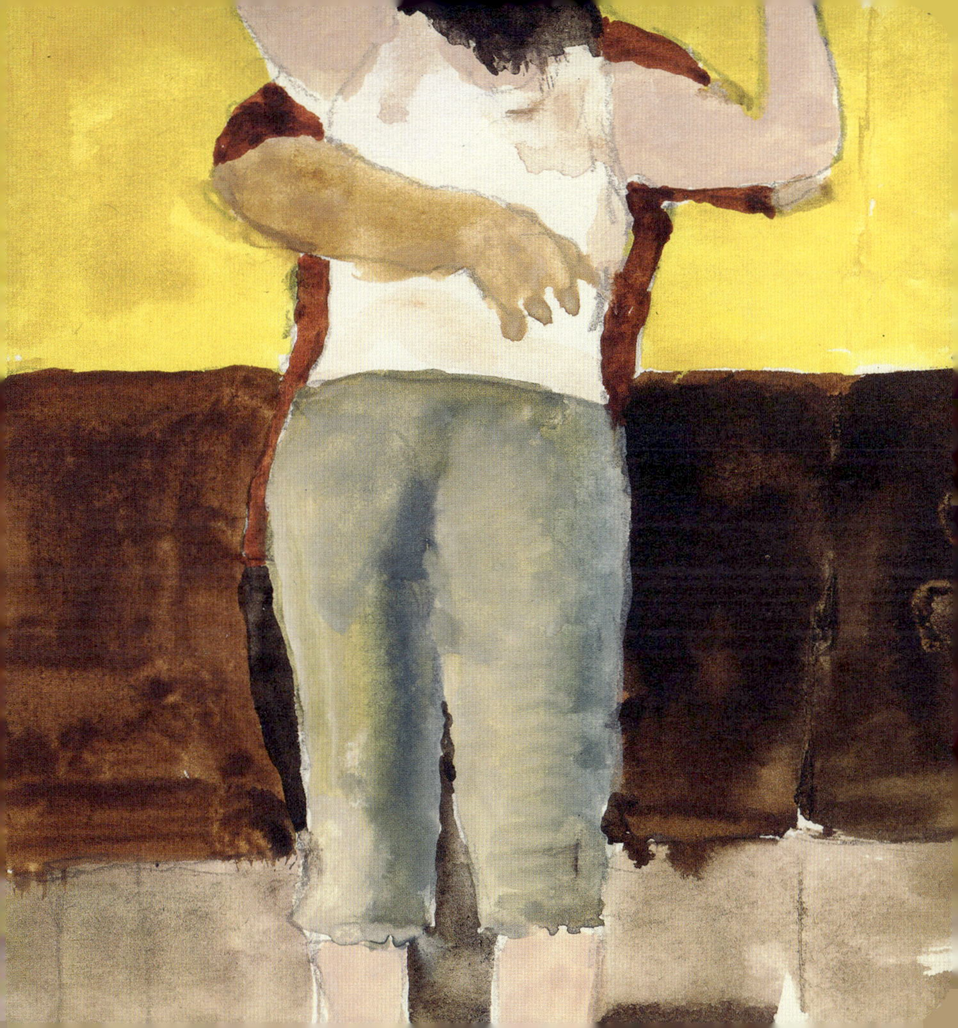

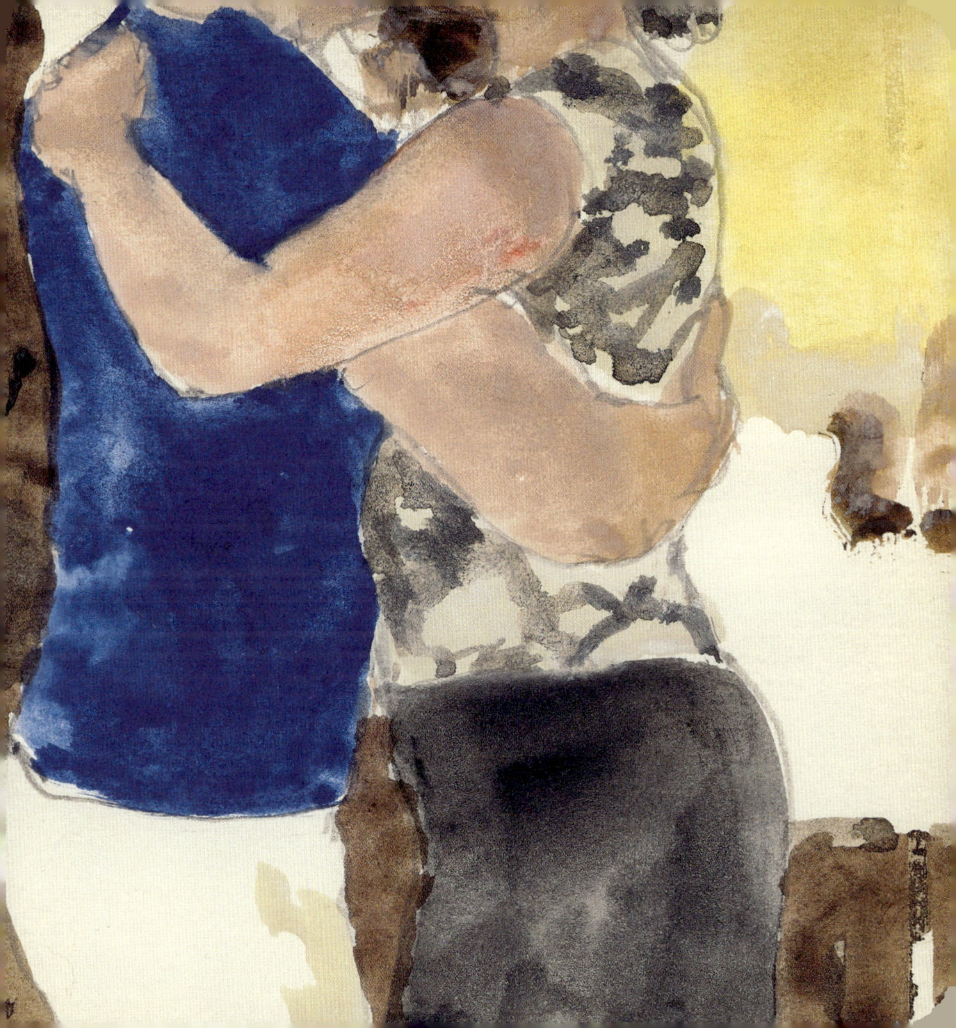

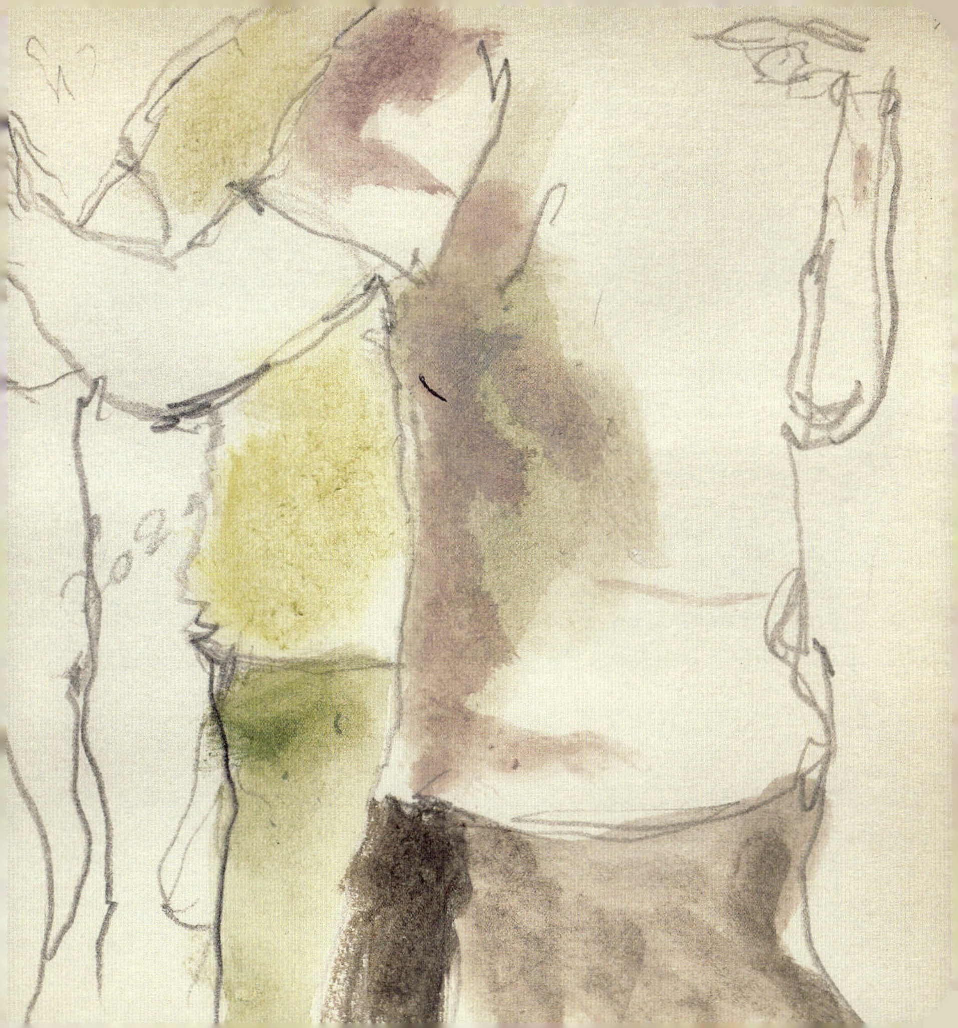

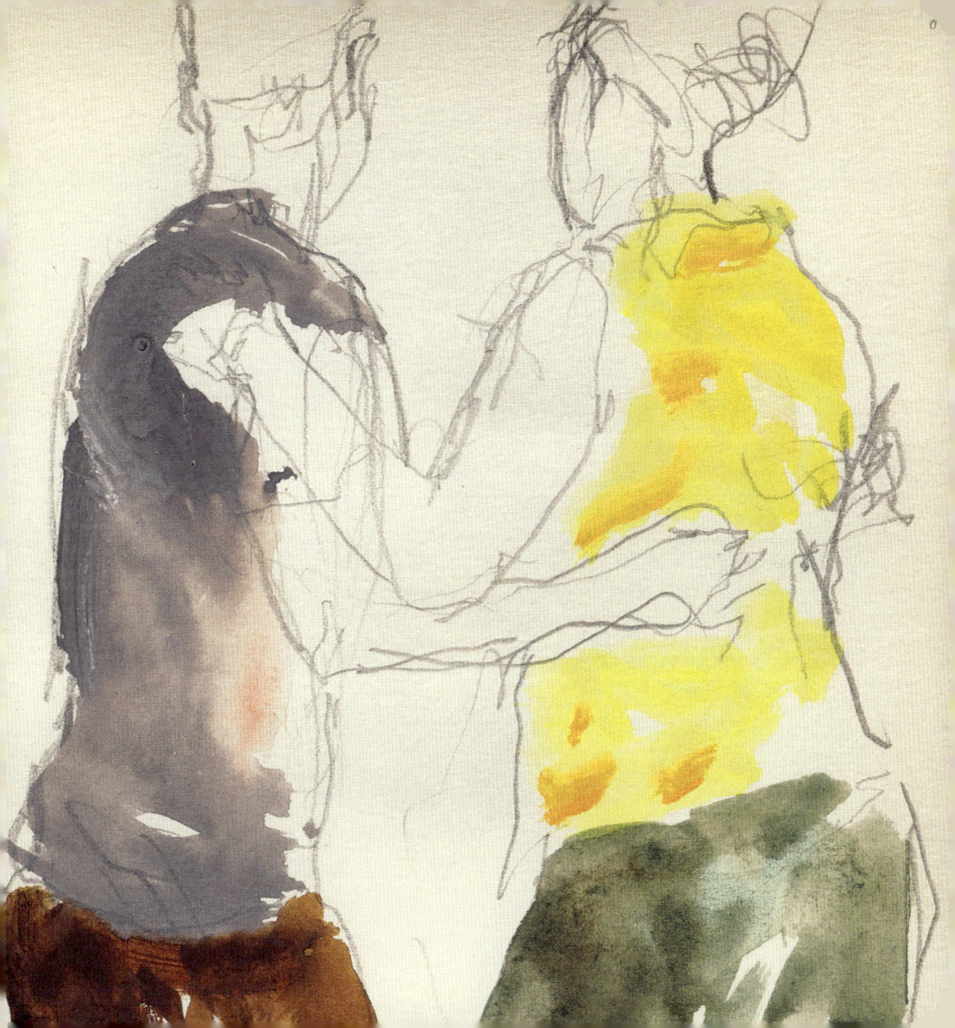

Monday 17th November

Nic o Več

Sunday 18

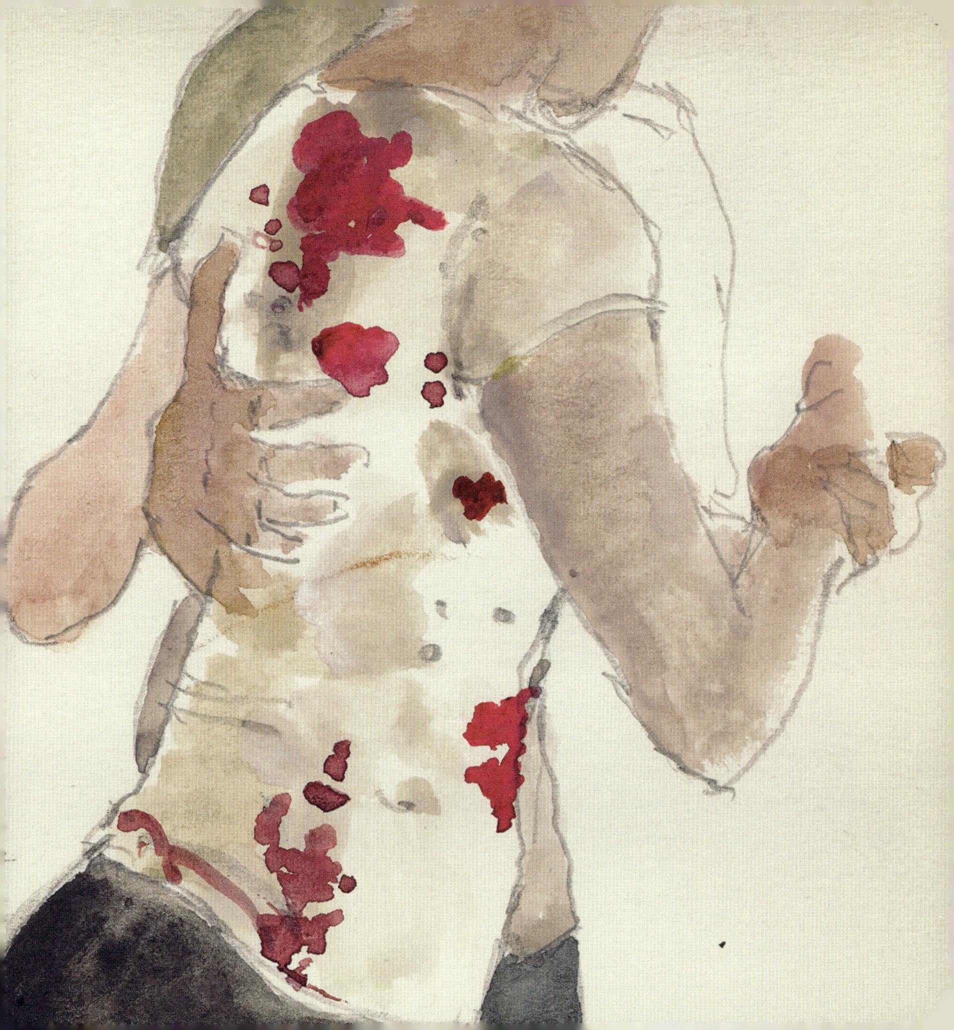

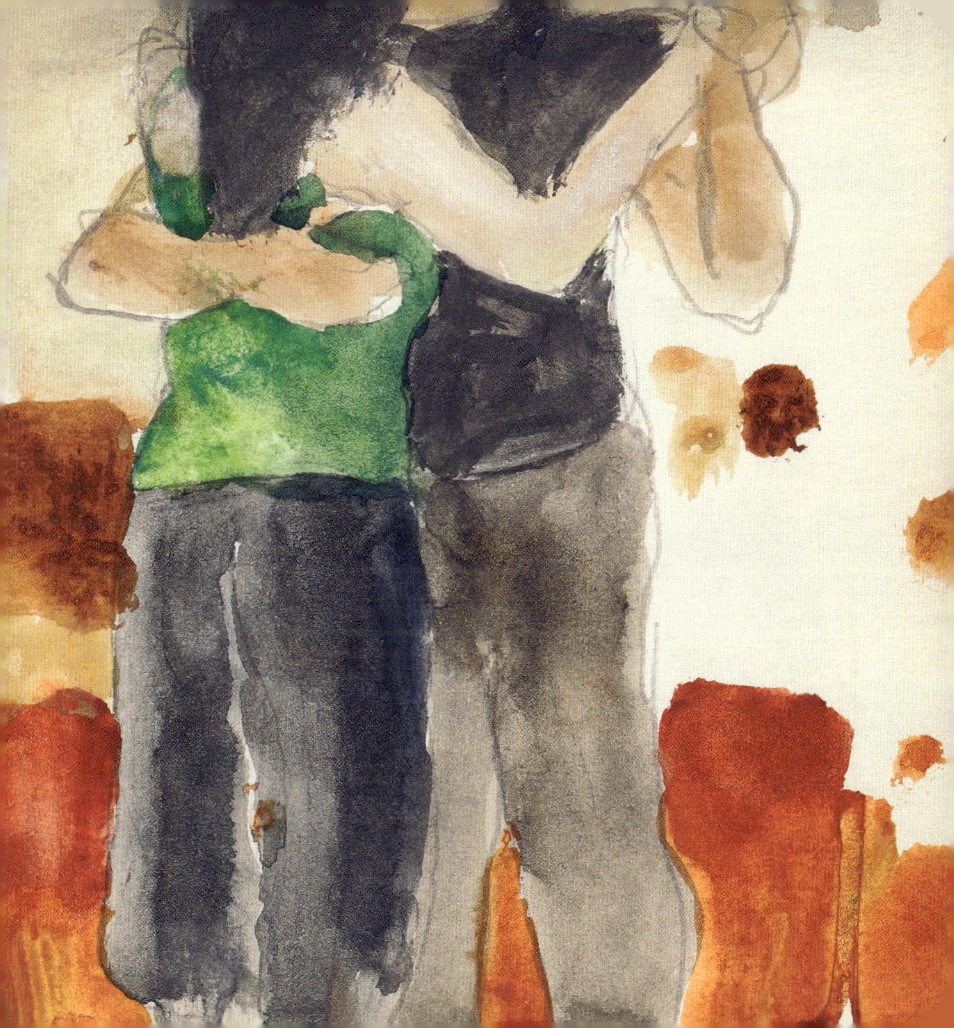

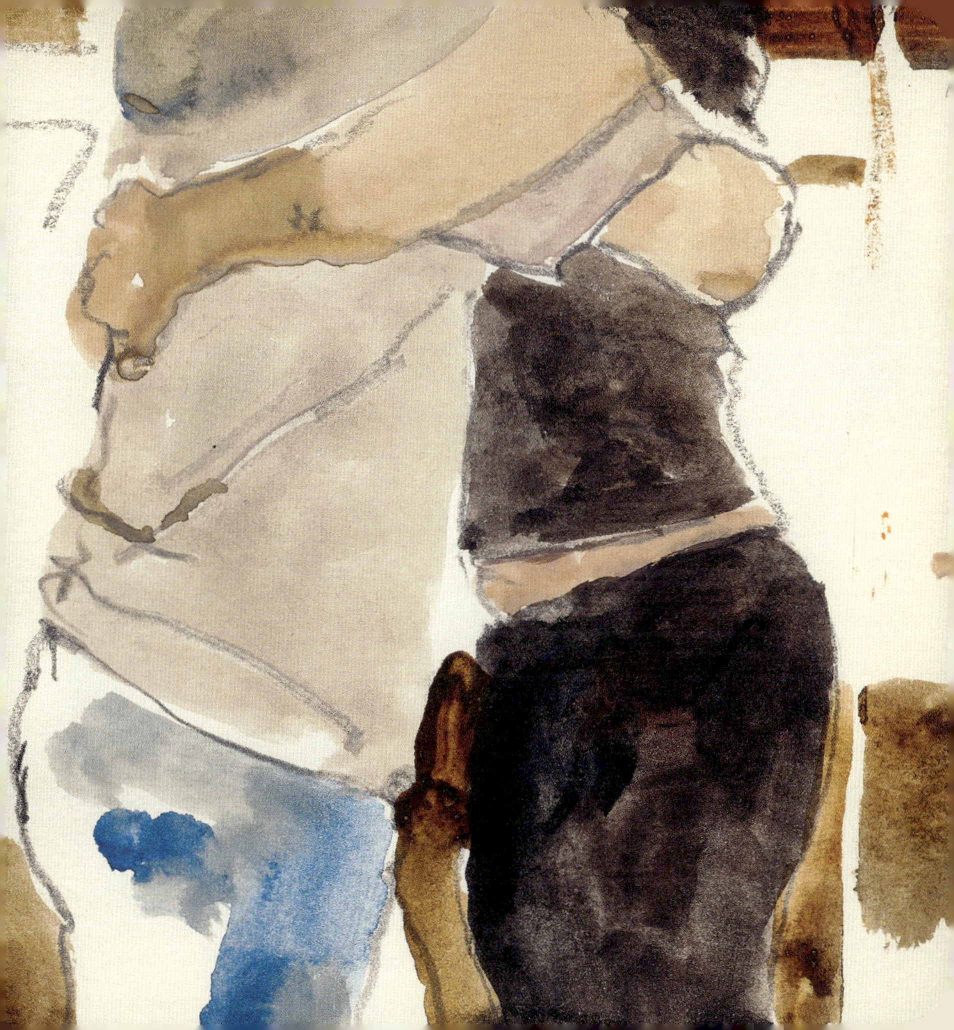

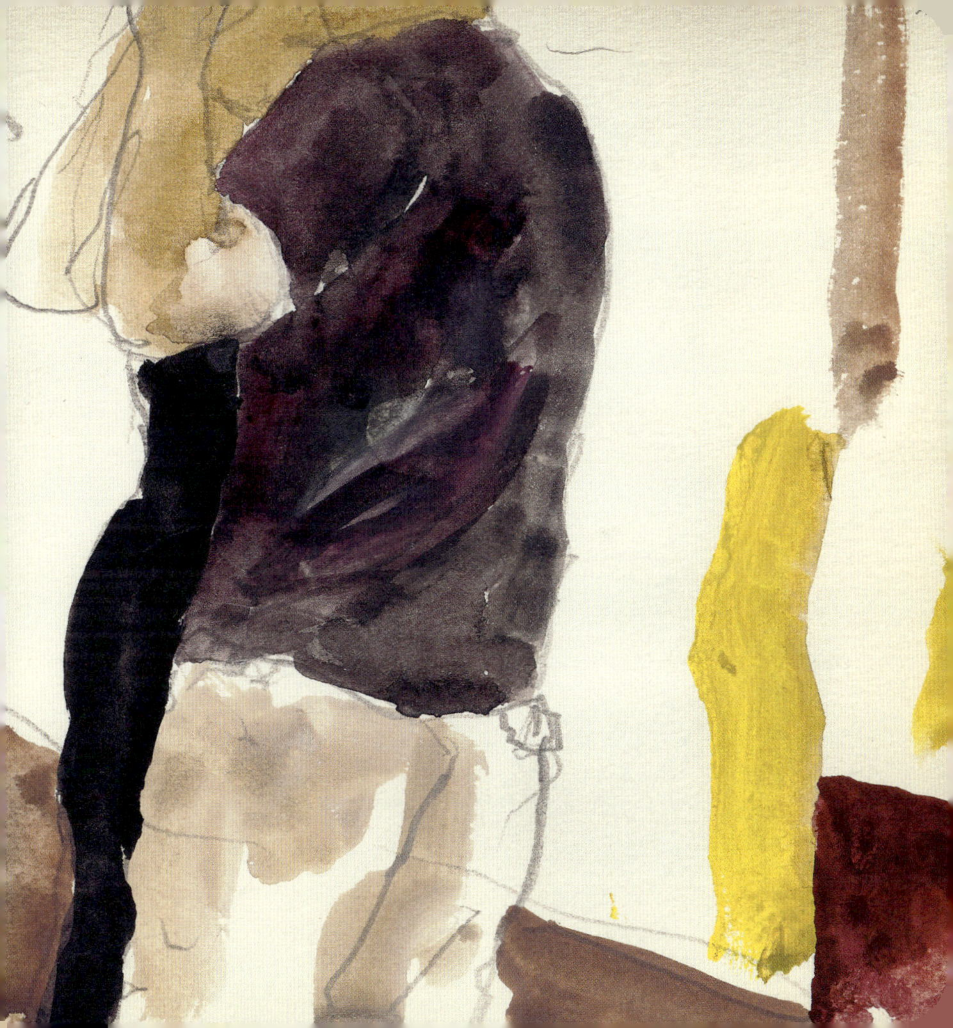

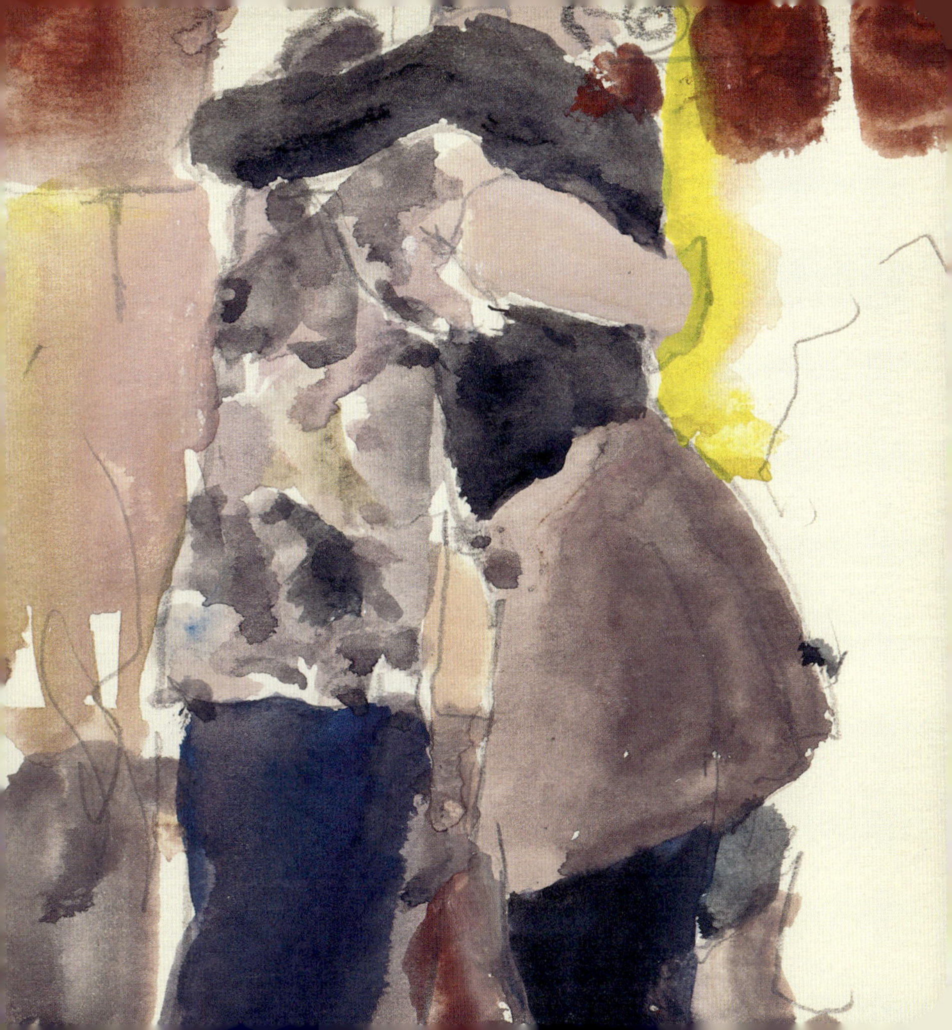

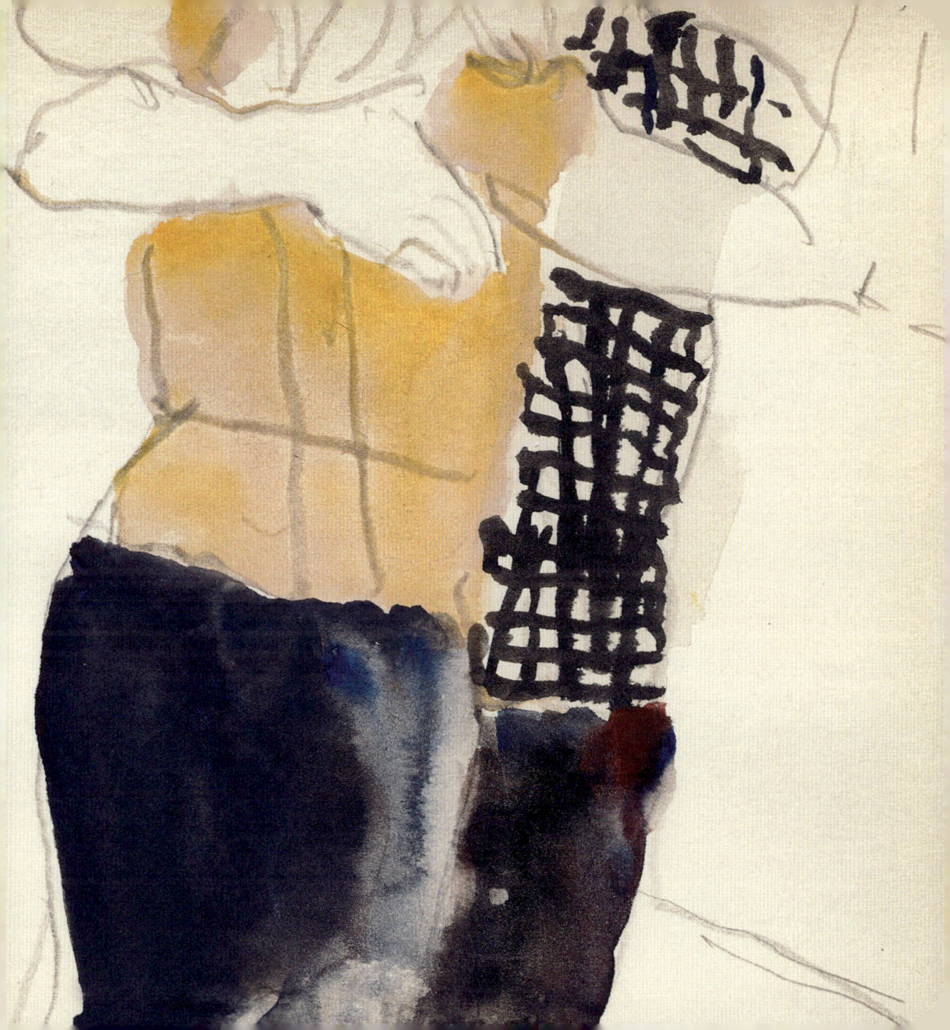

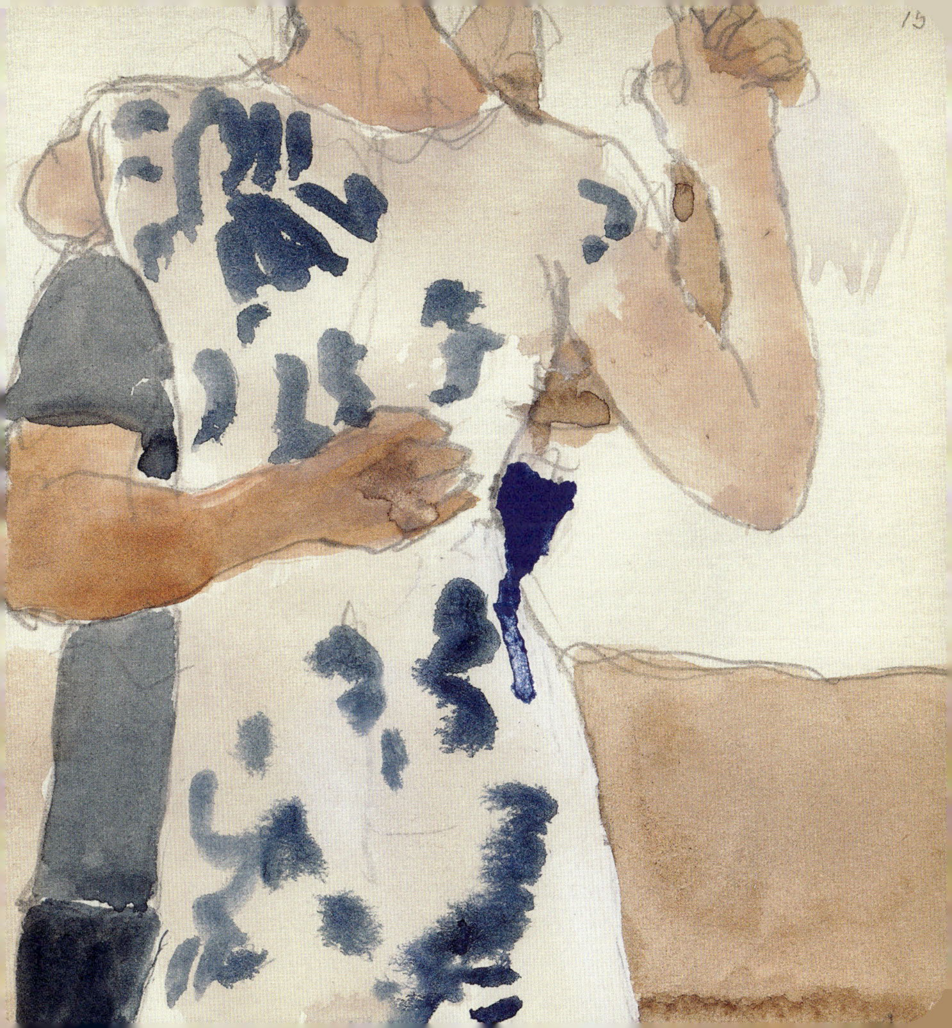
15

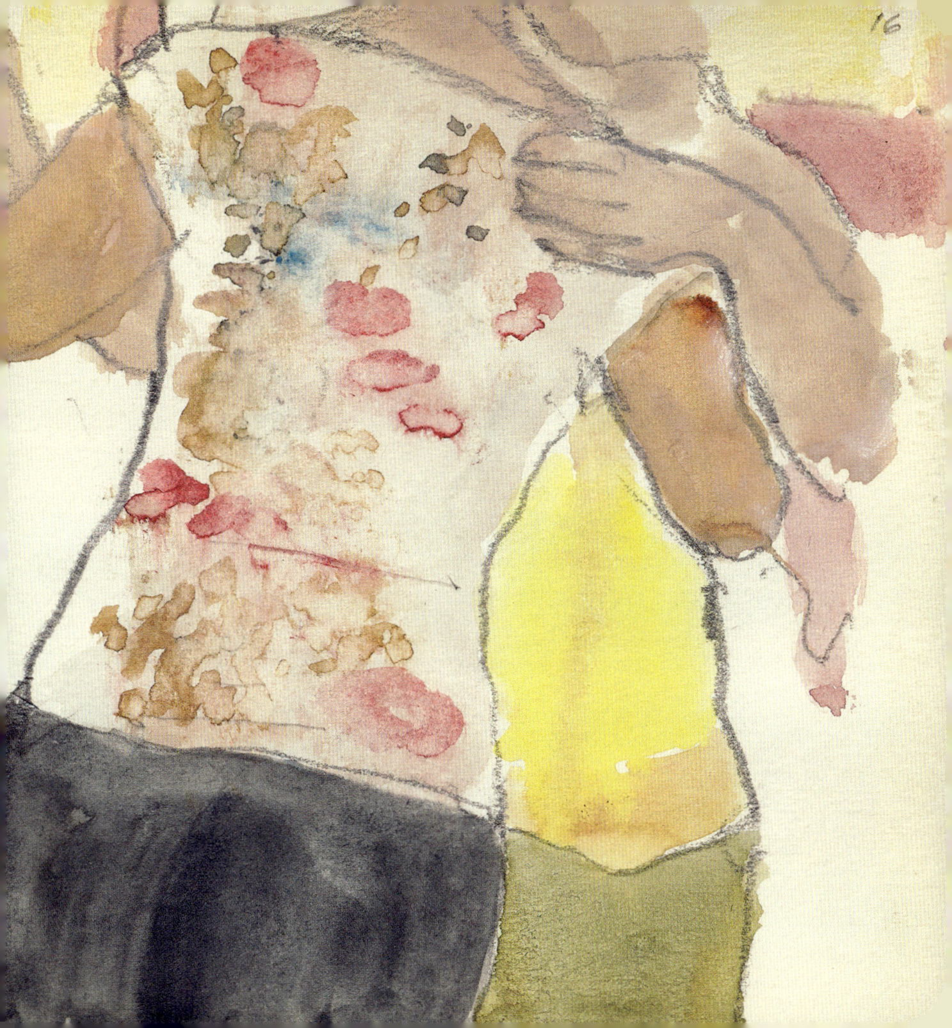
16

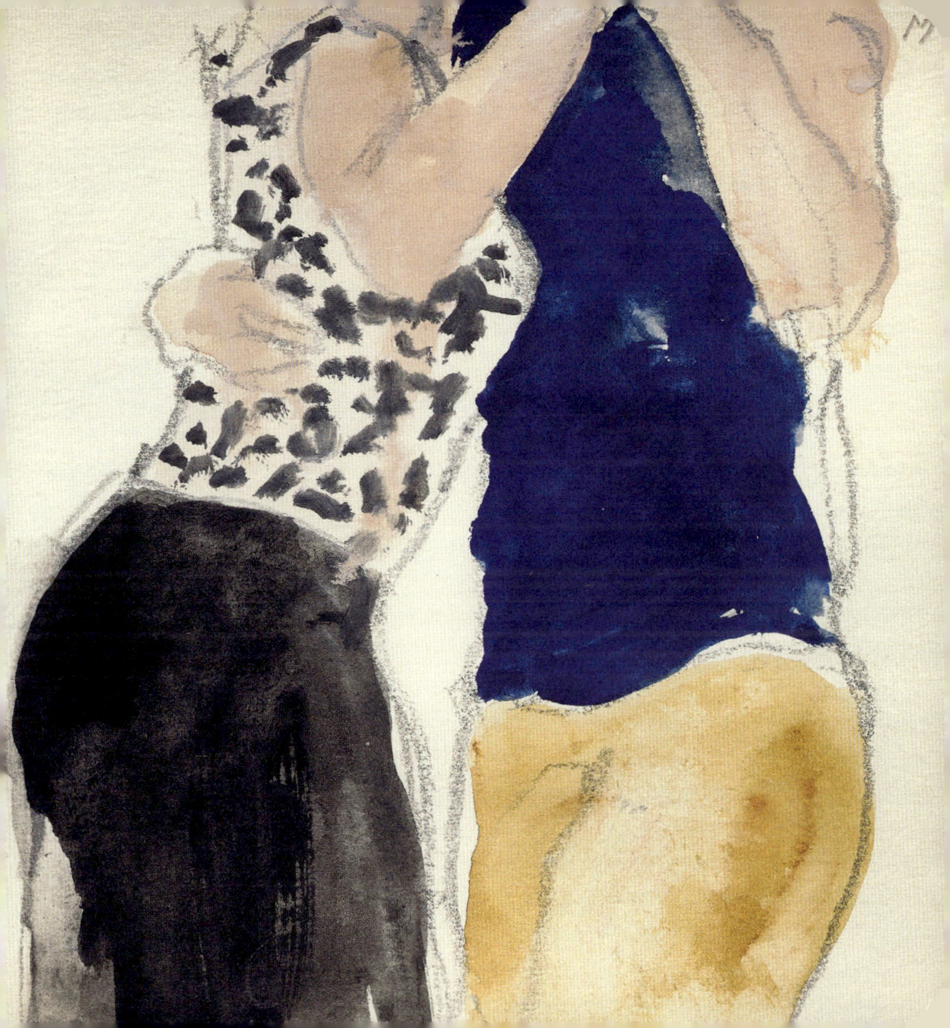

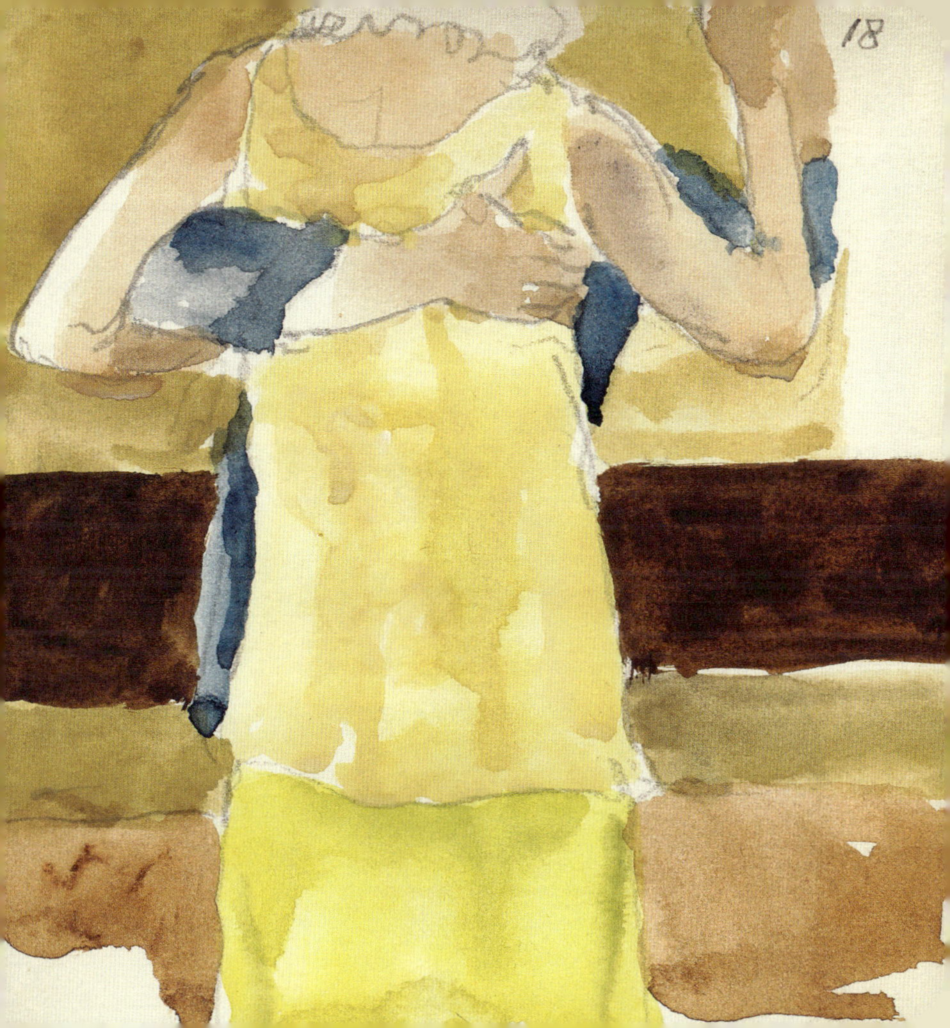
18

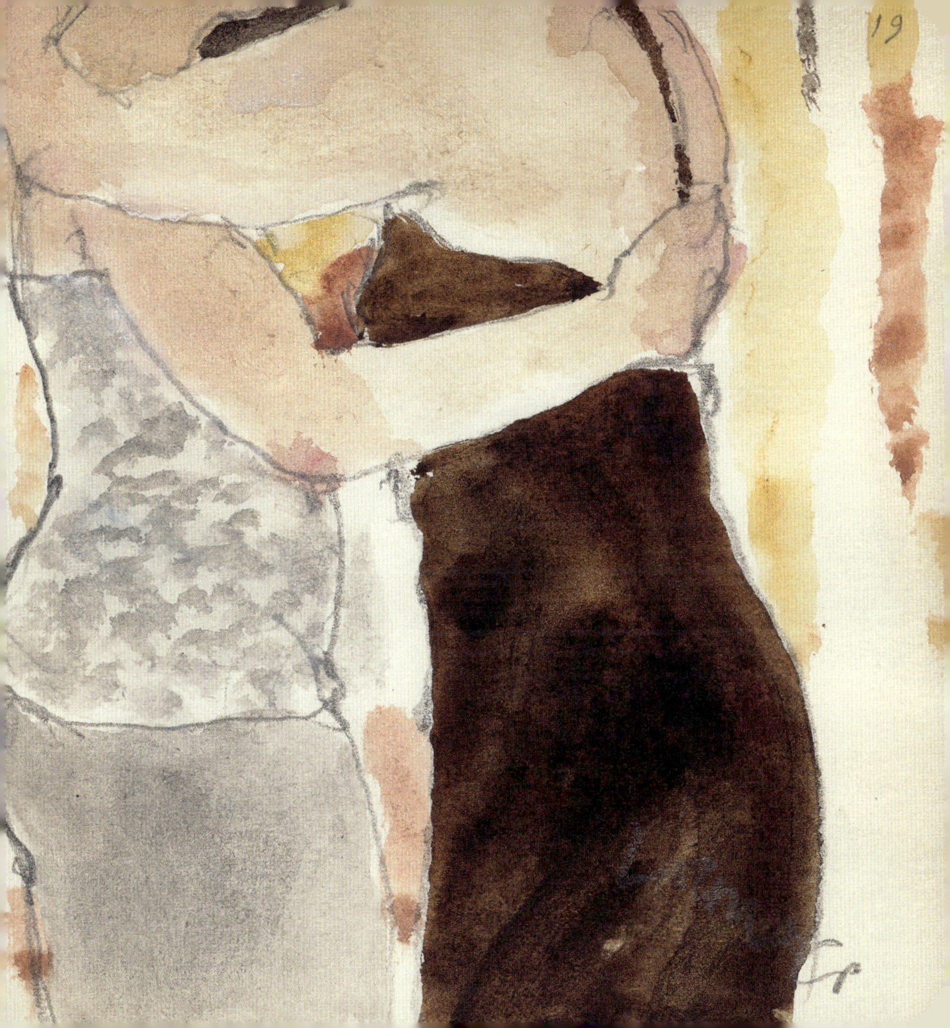

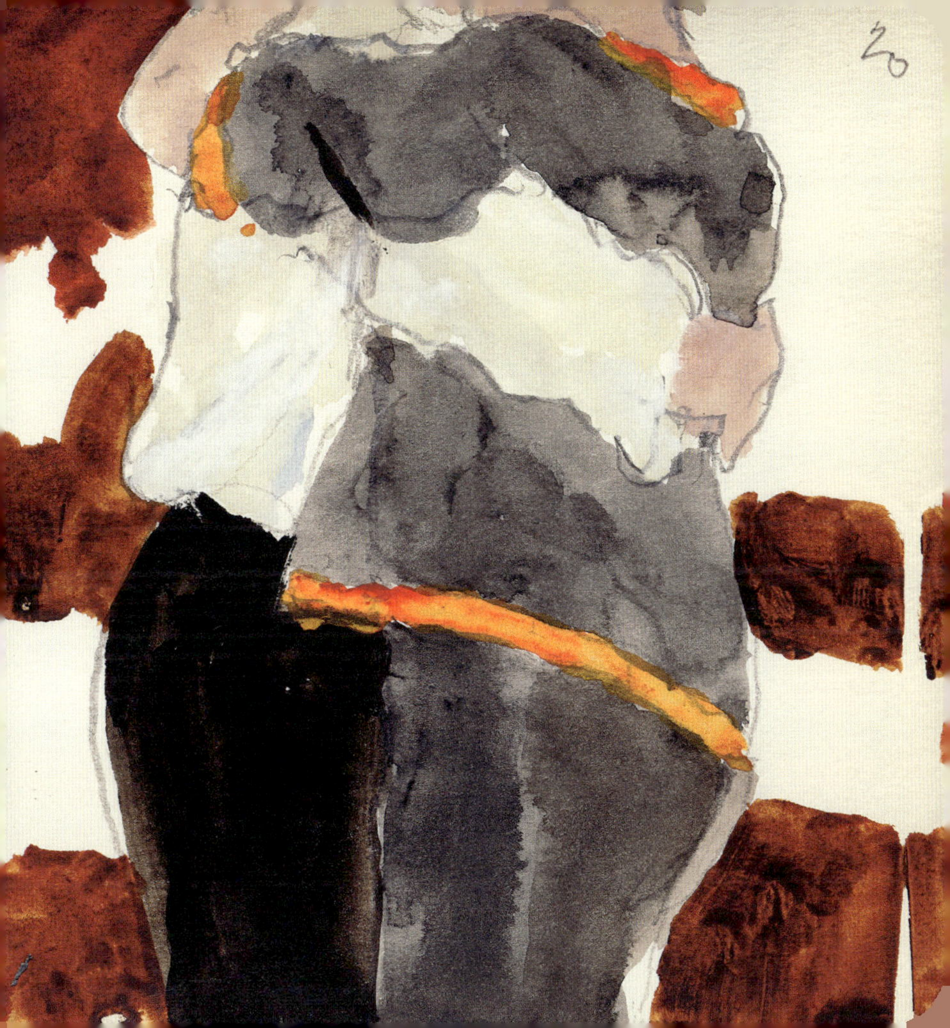
20

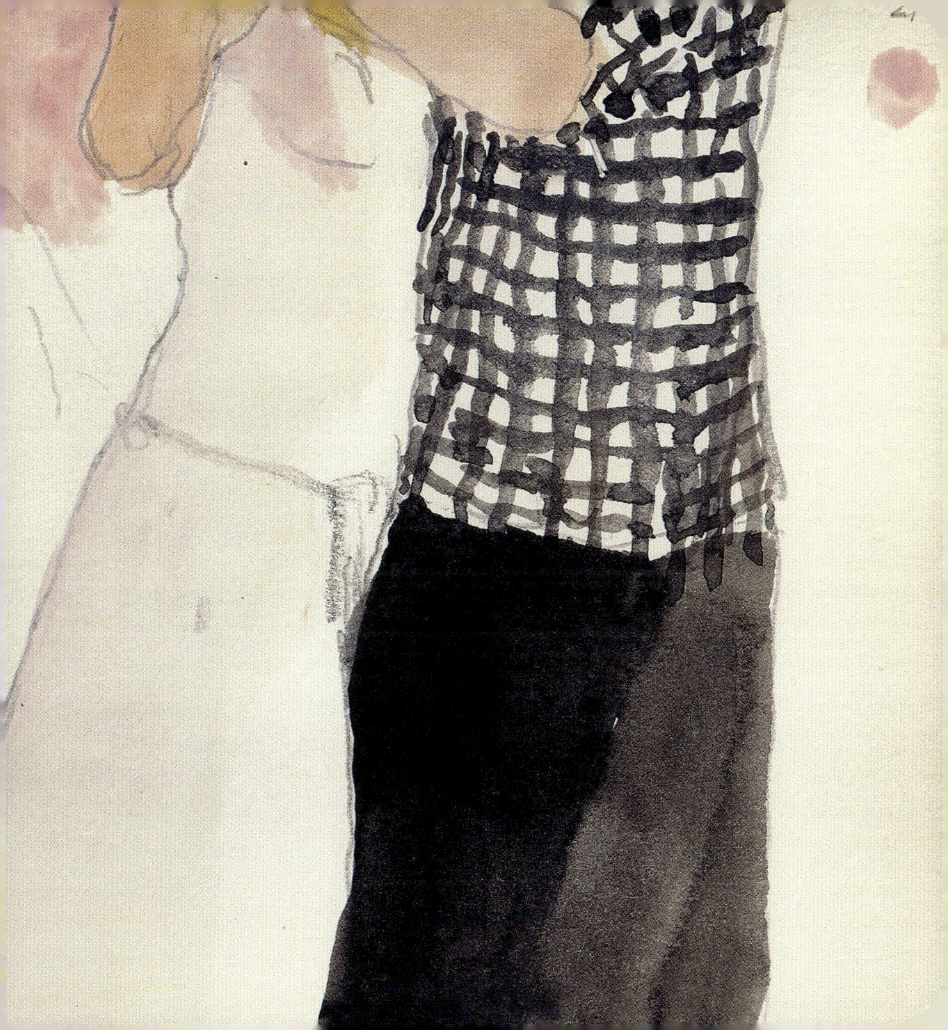

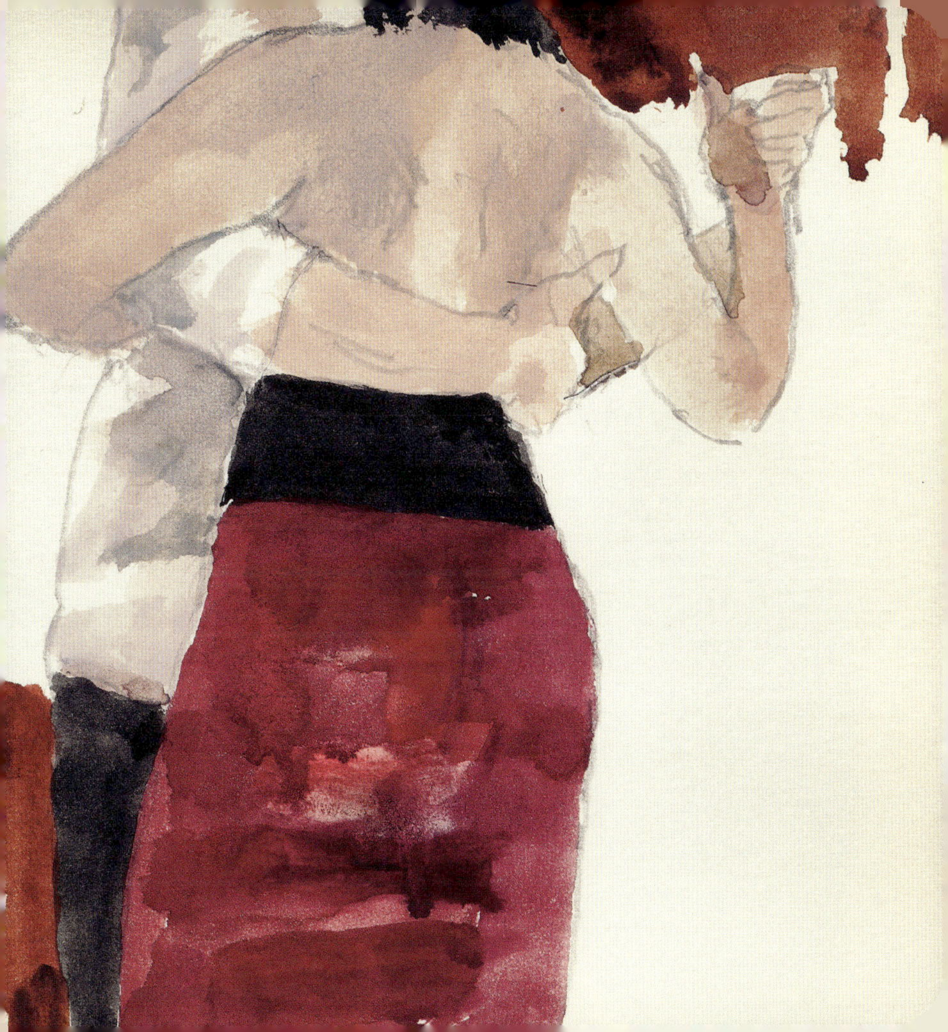

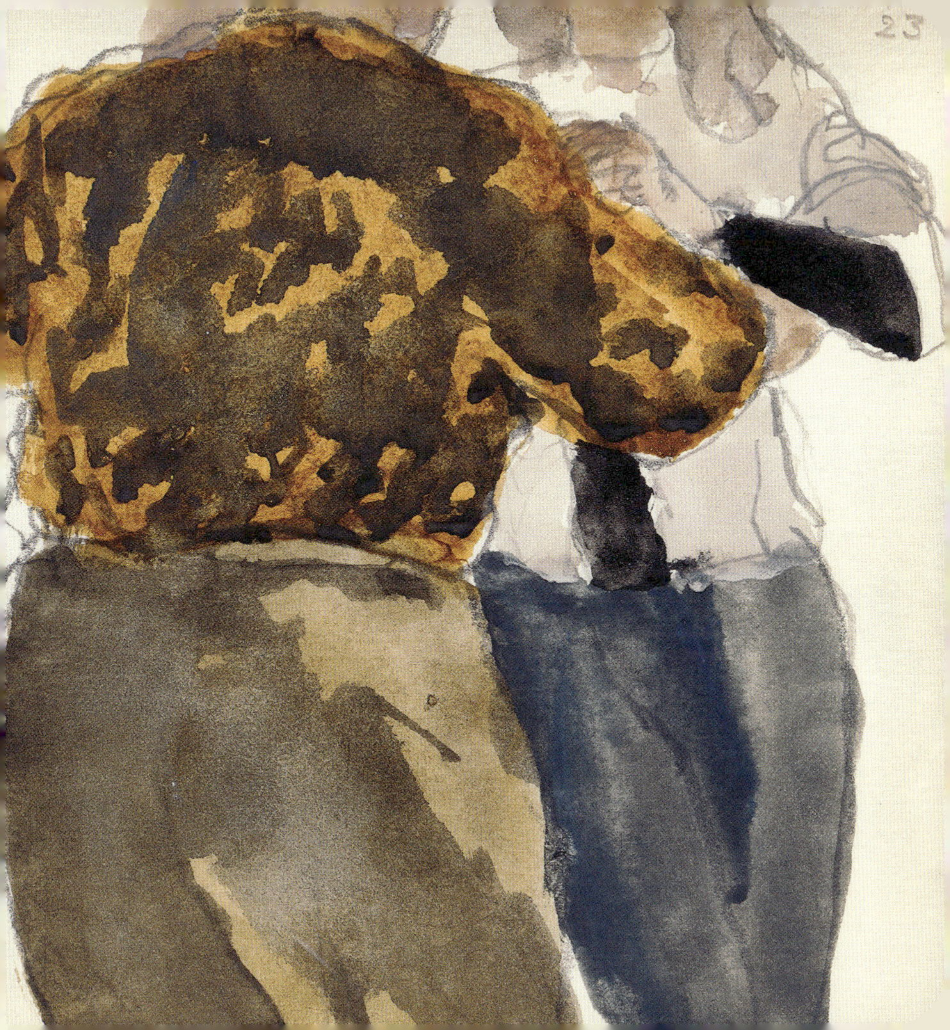
23

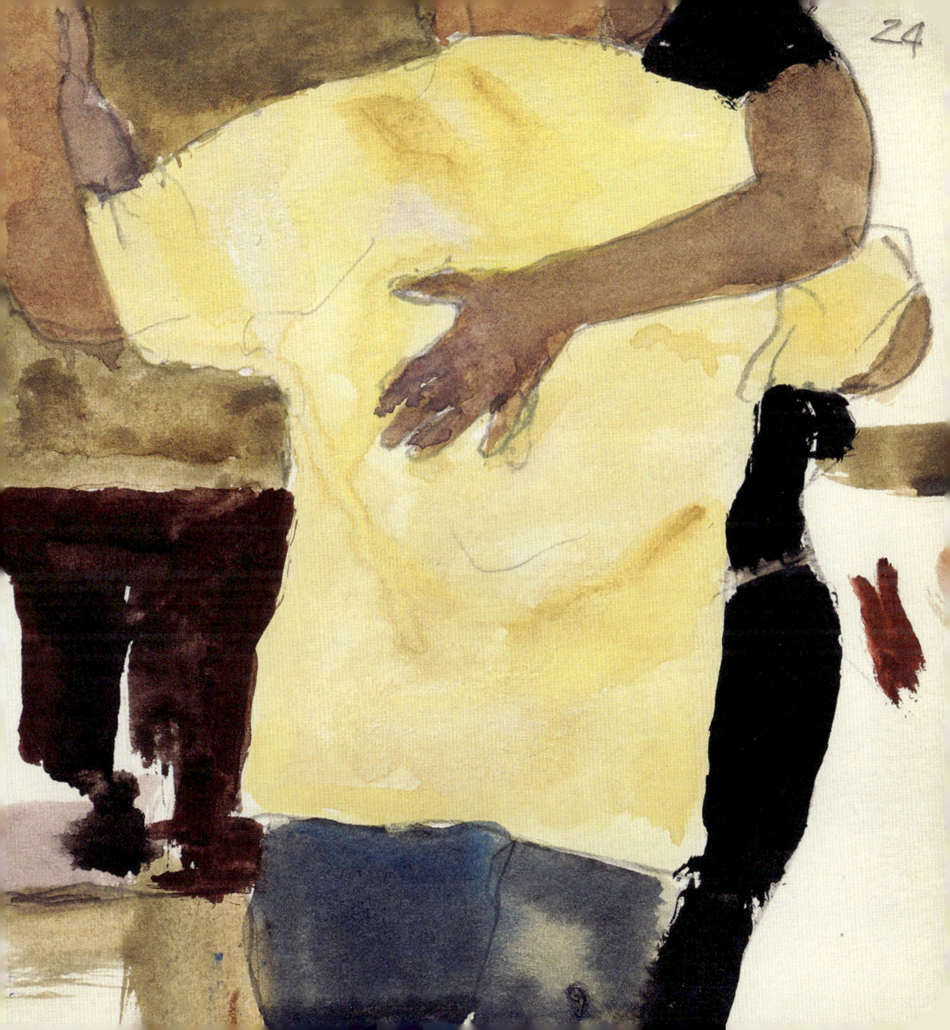
24

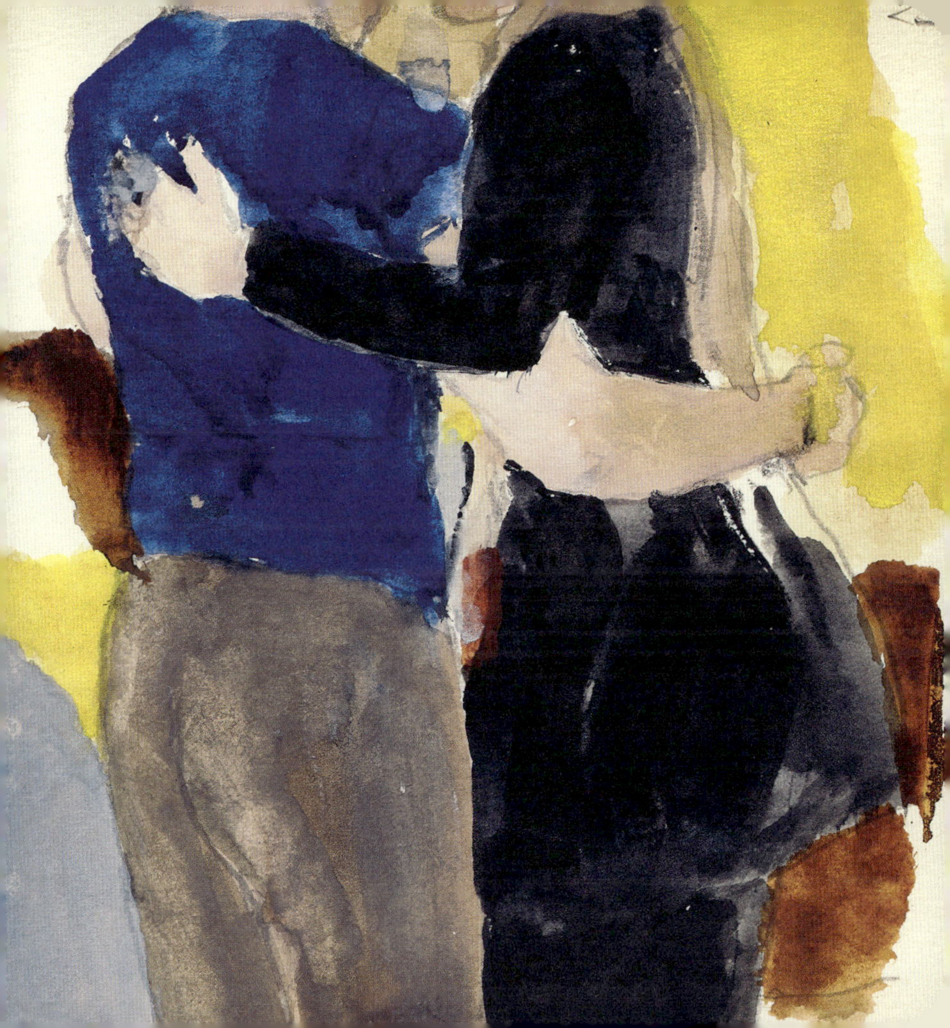

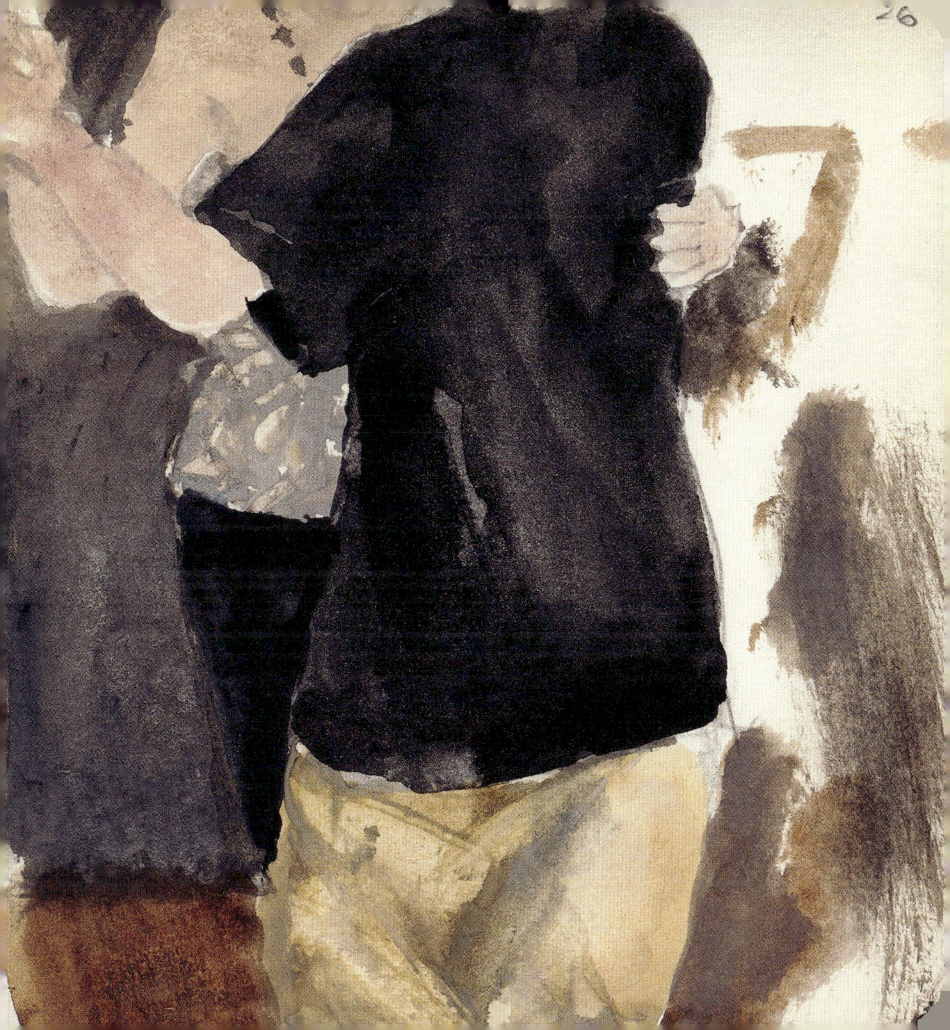
26

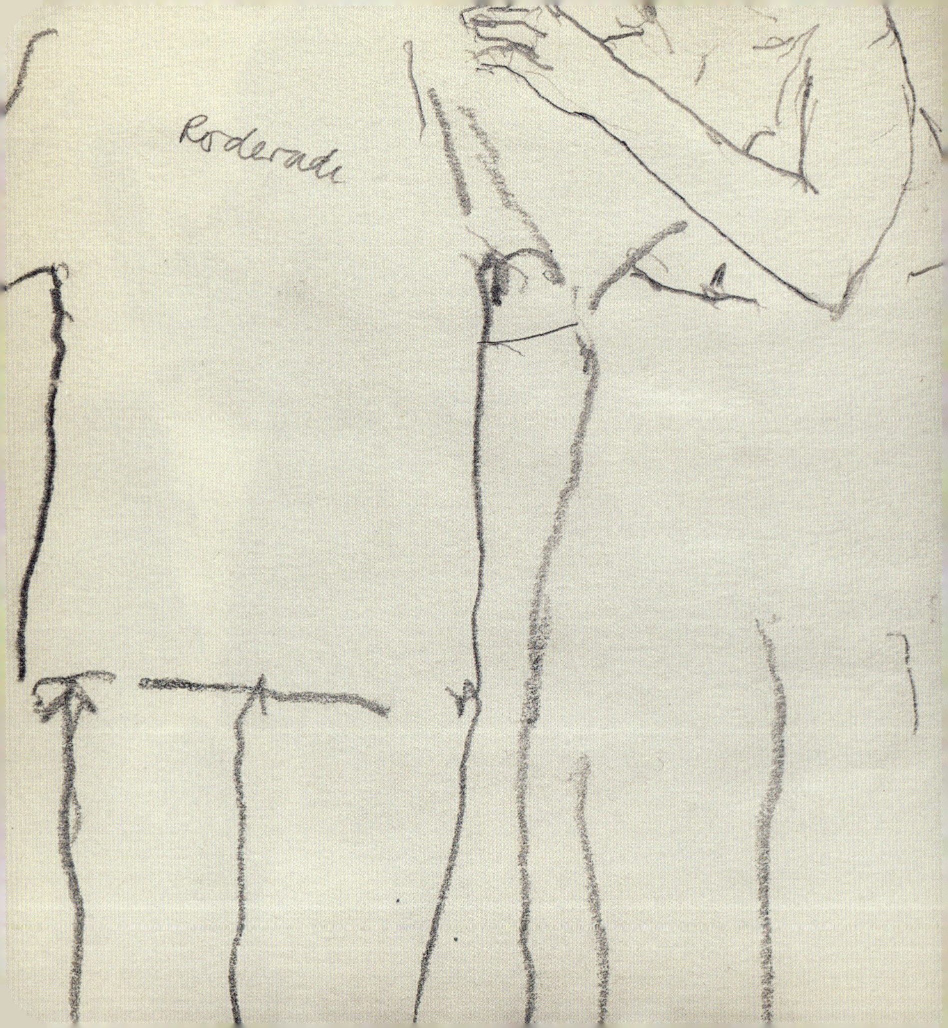
Roderade

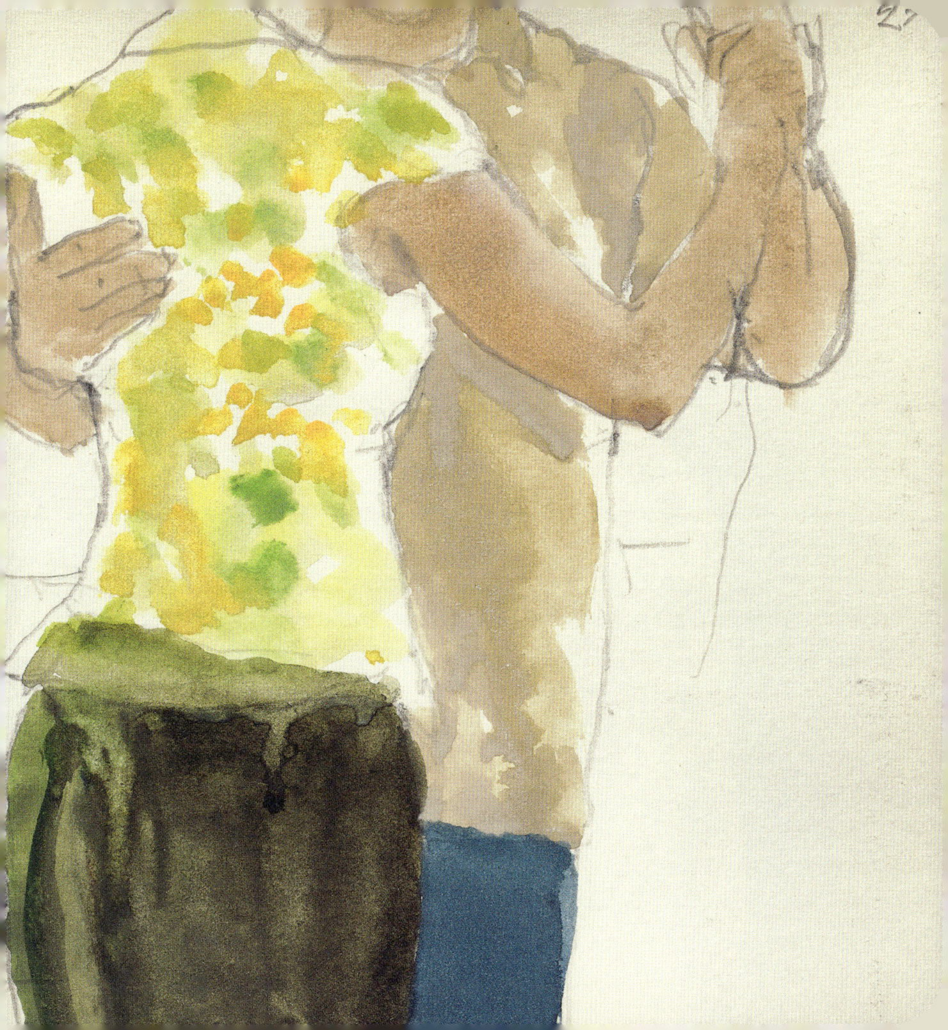

Dove Merce Roderdez.

Marion moore Poet

D'veglian

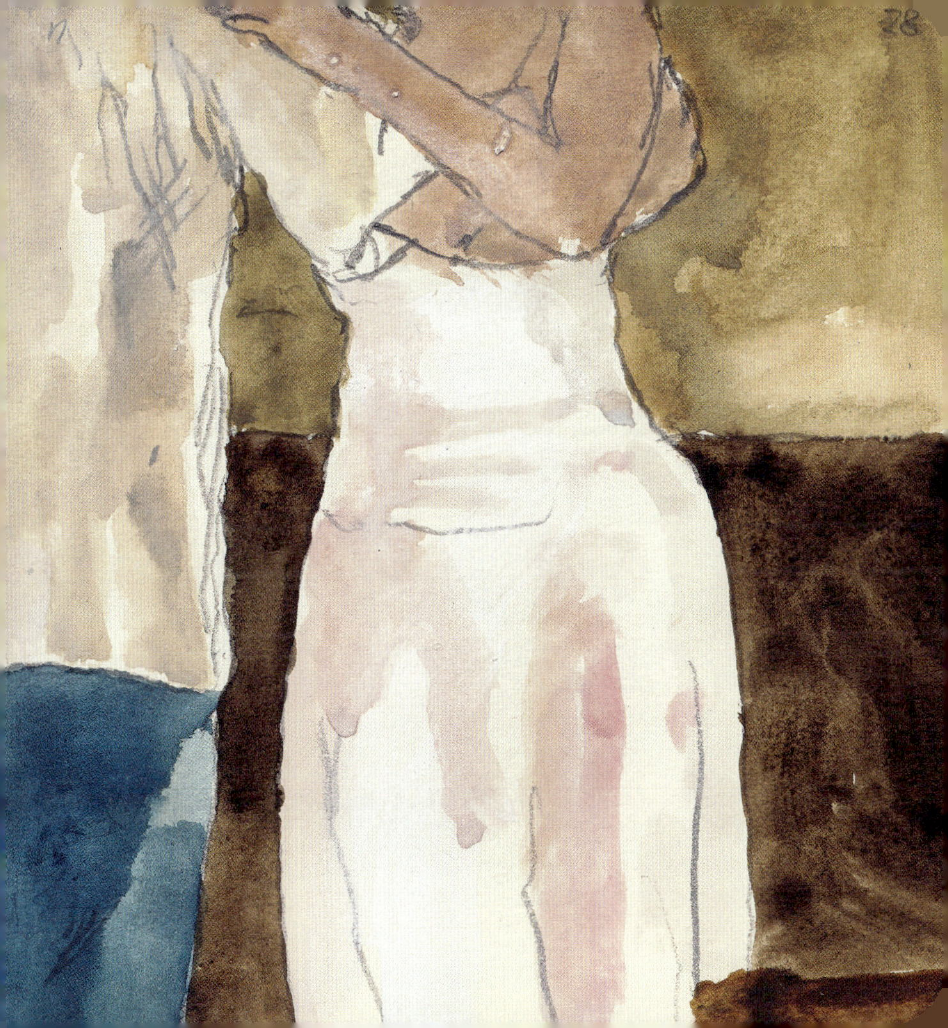
28

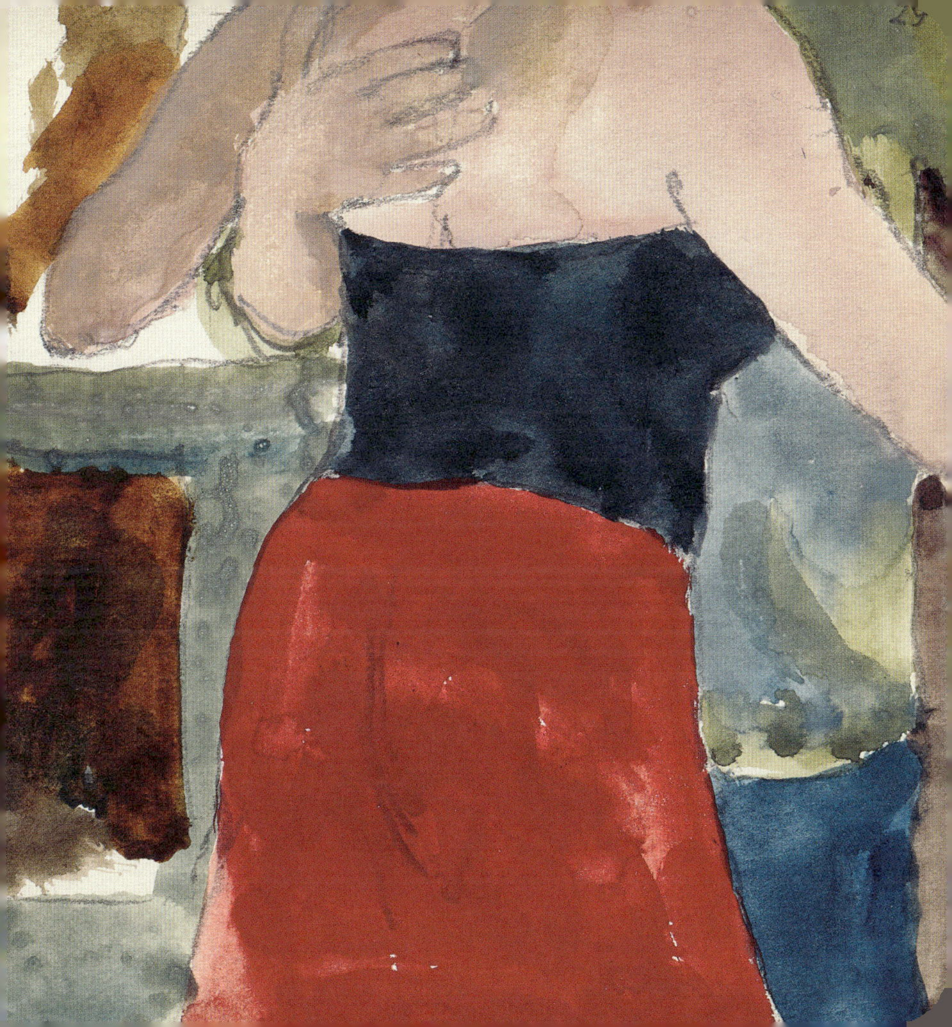

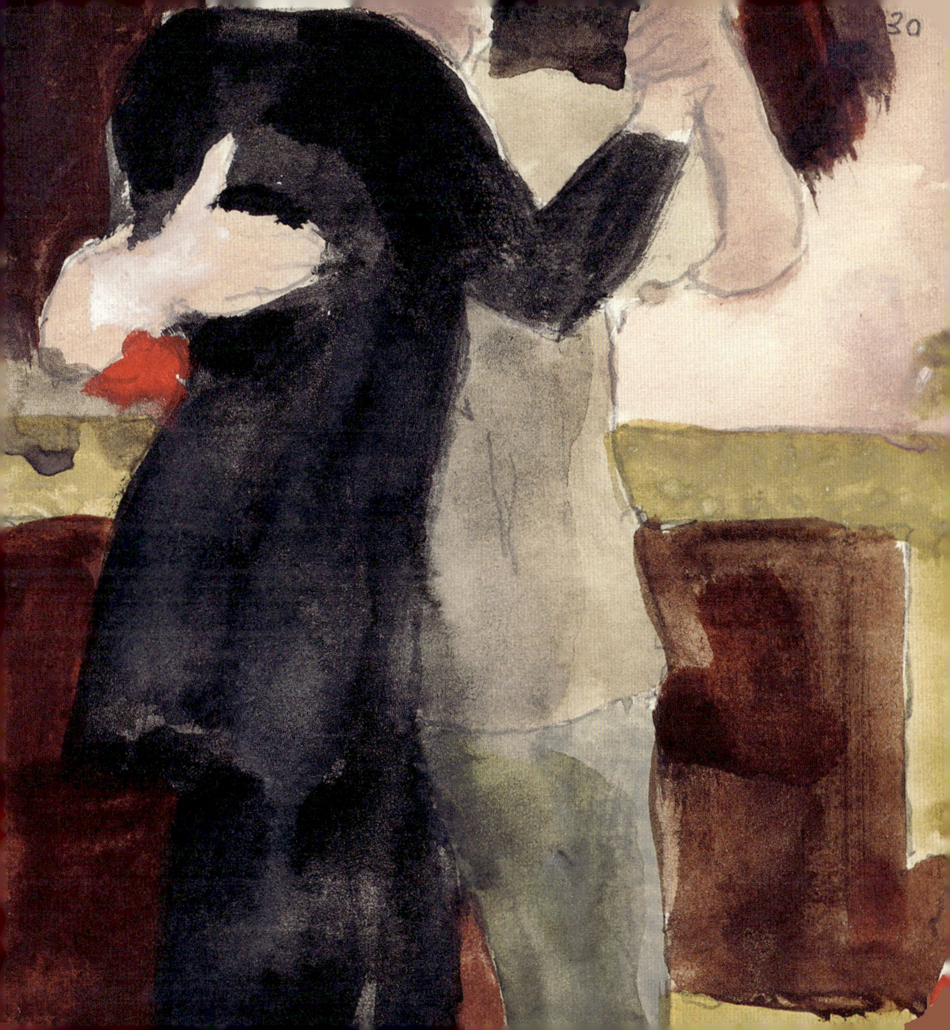
30

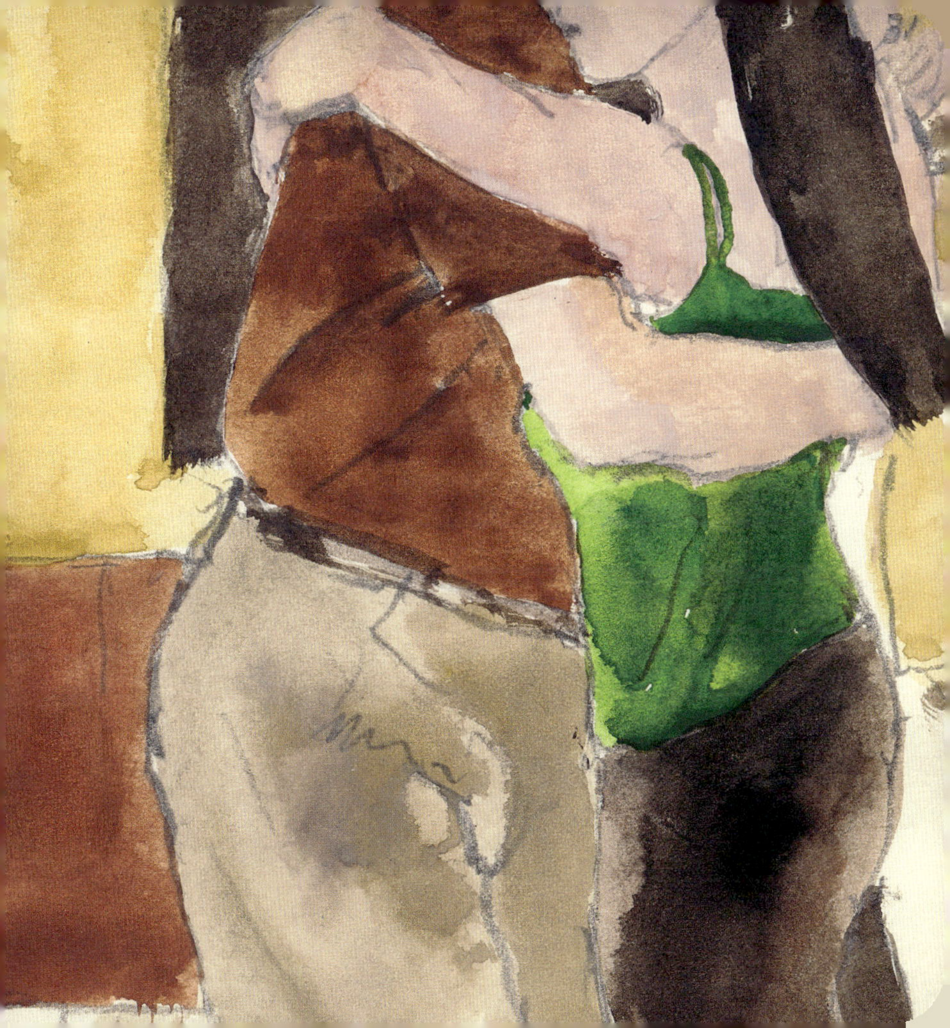

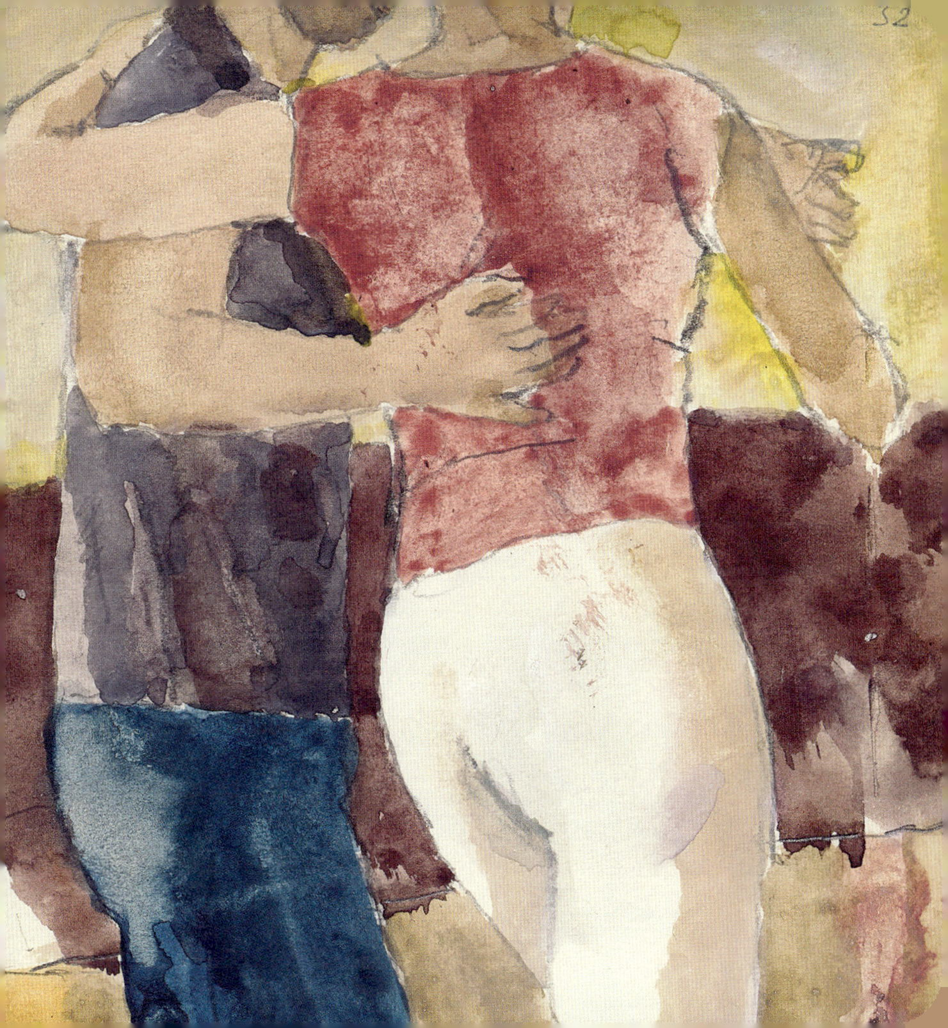
52

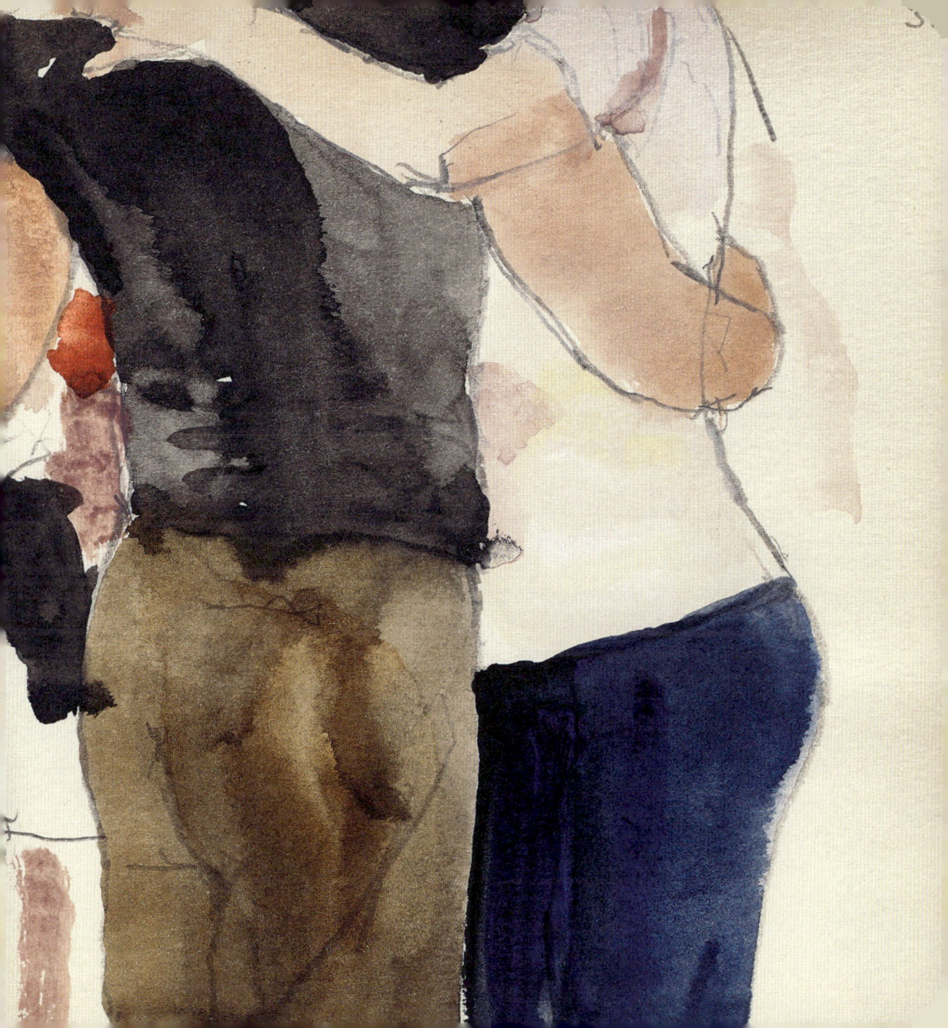

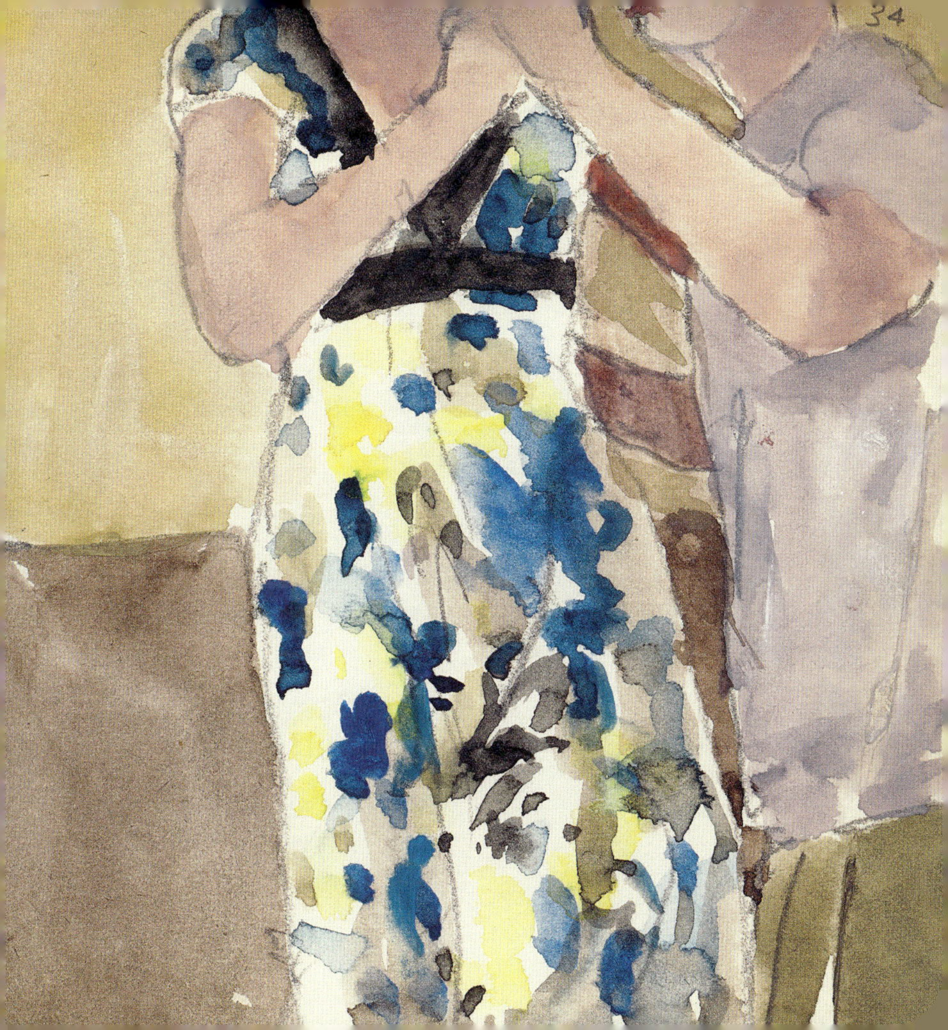
34

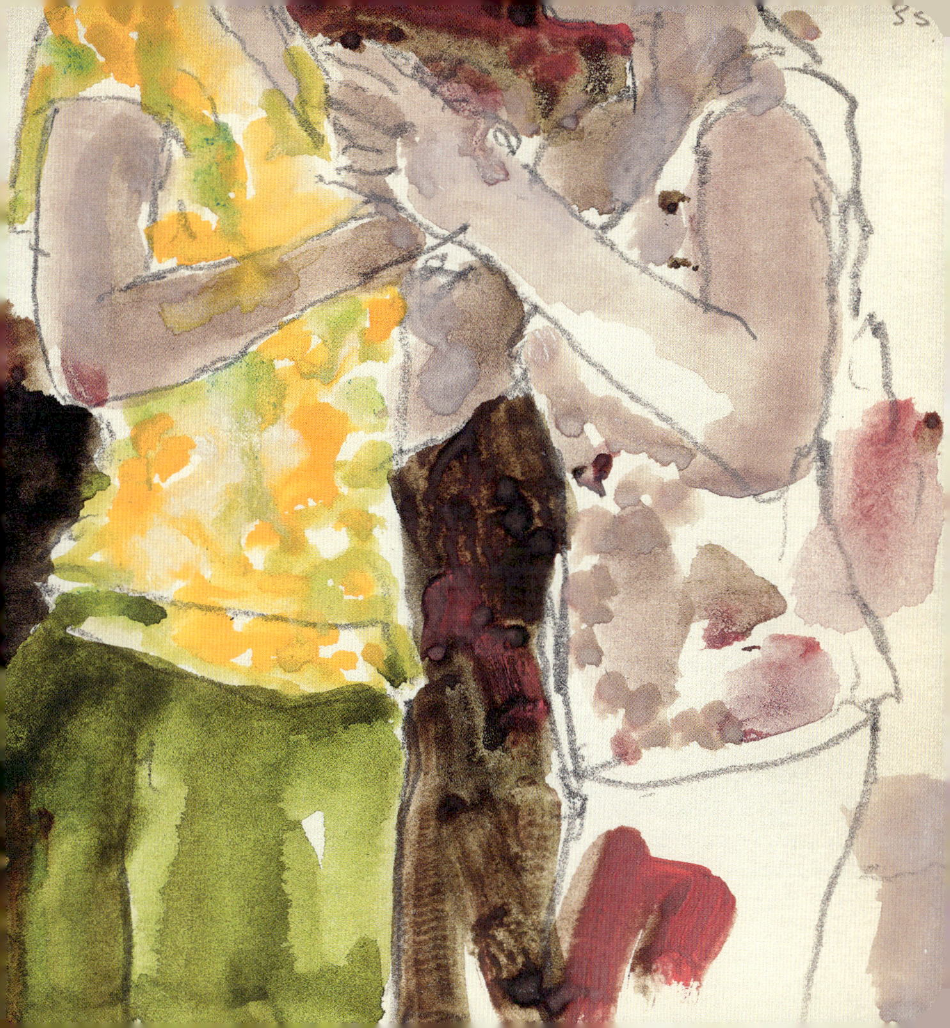

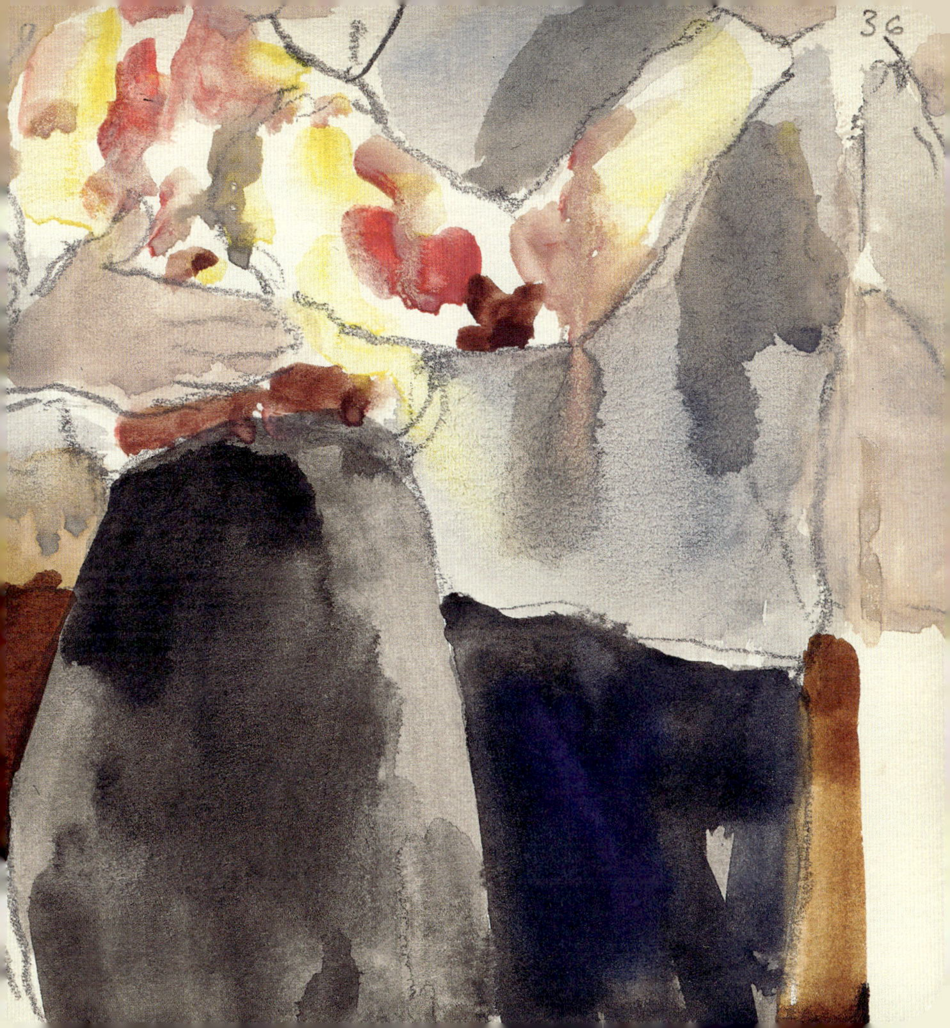
36

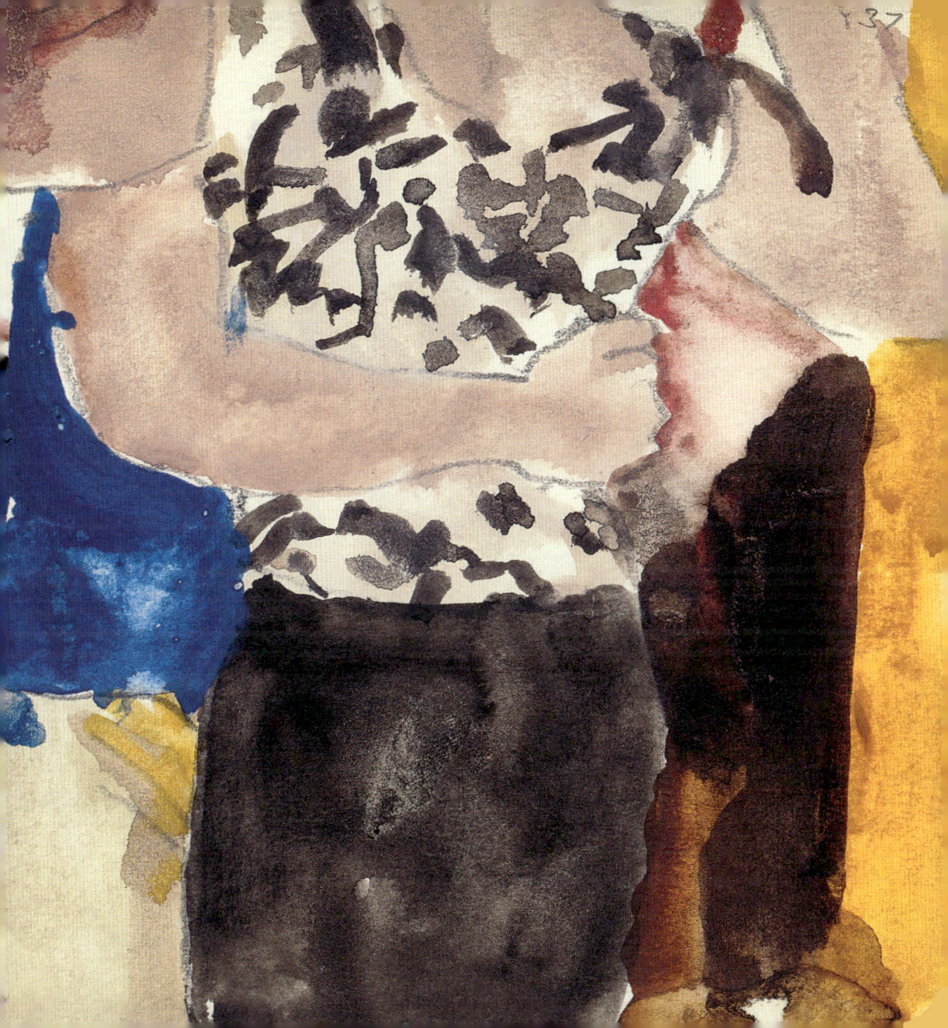

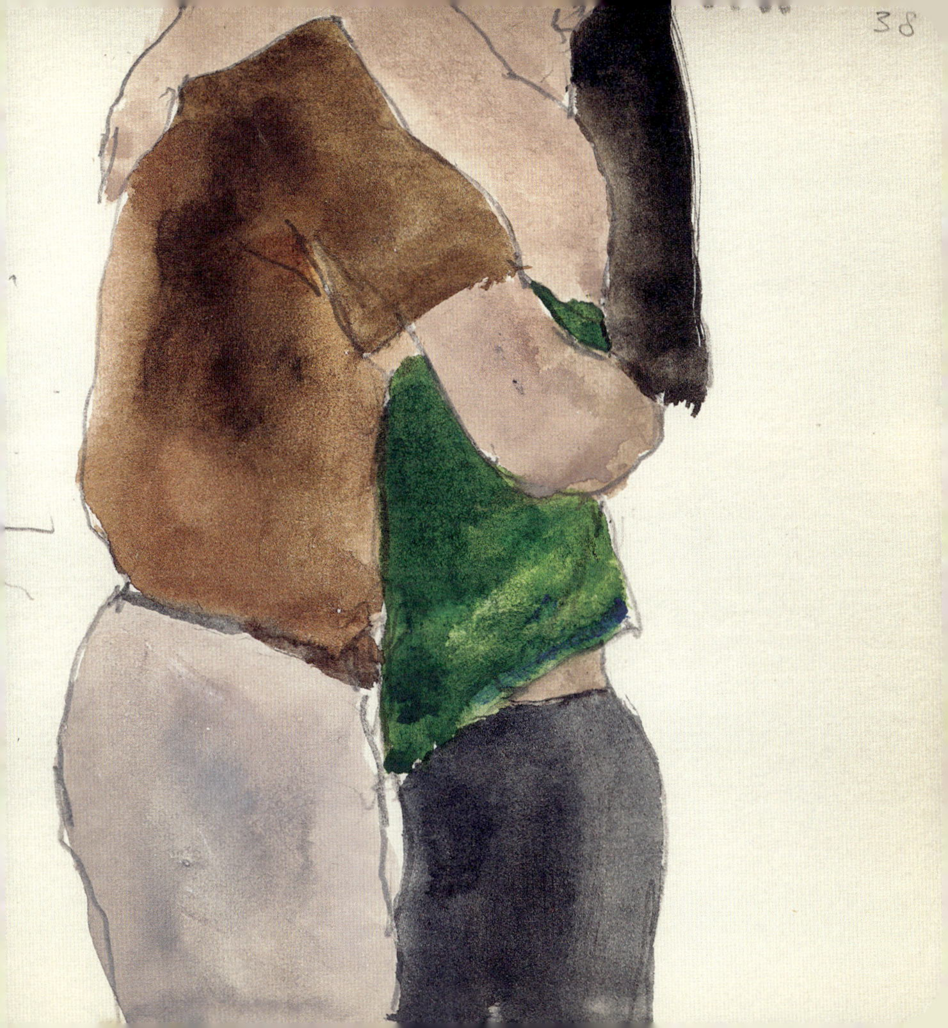
38

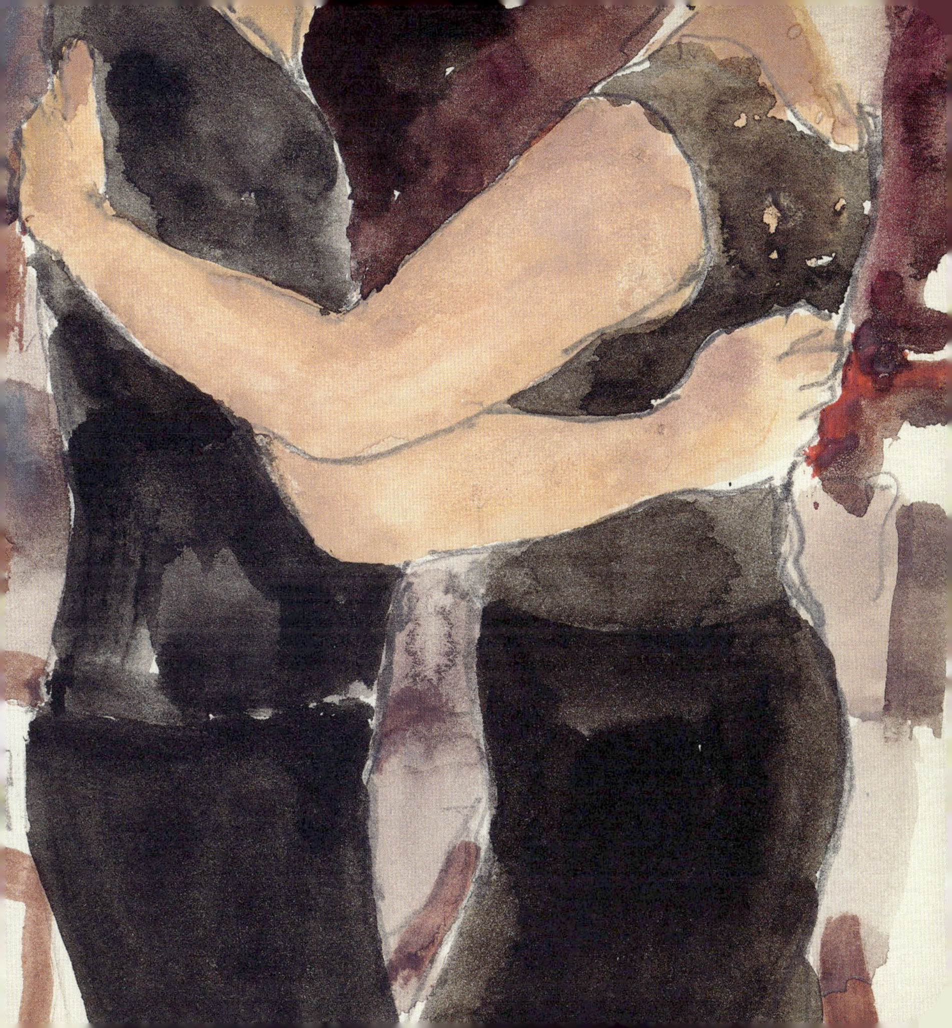

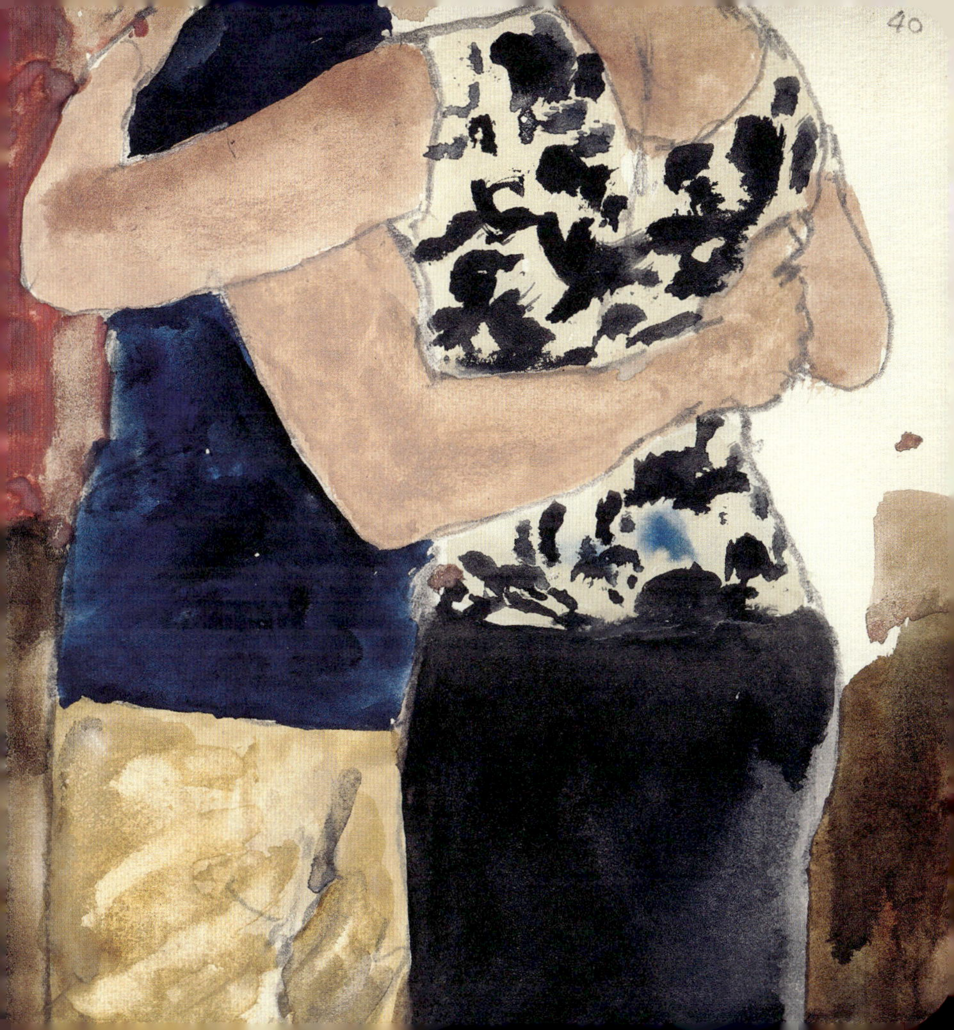
40

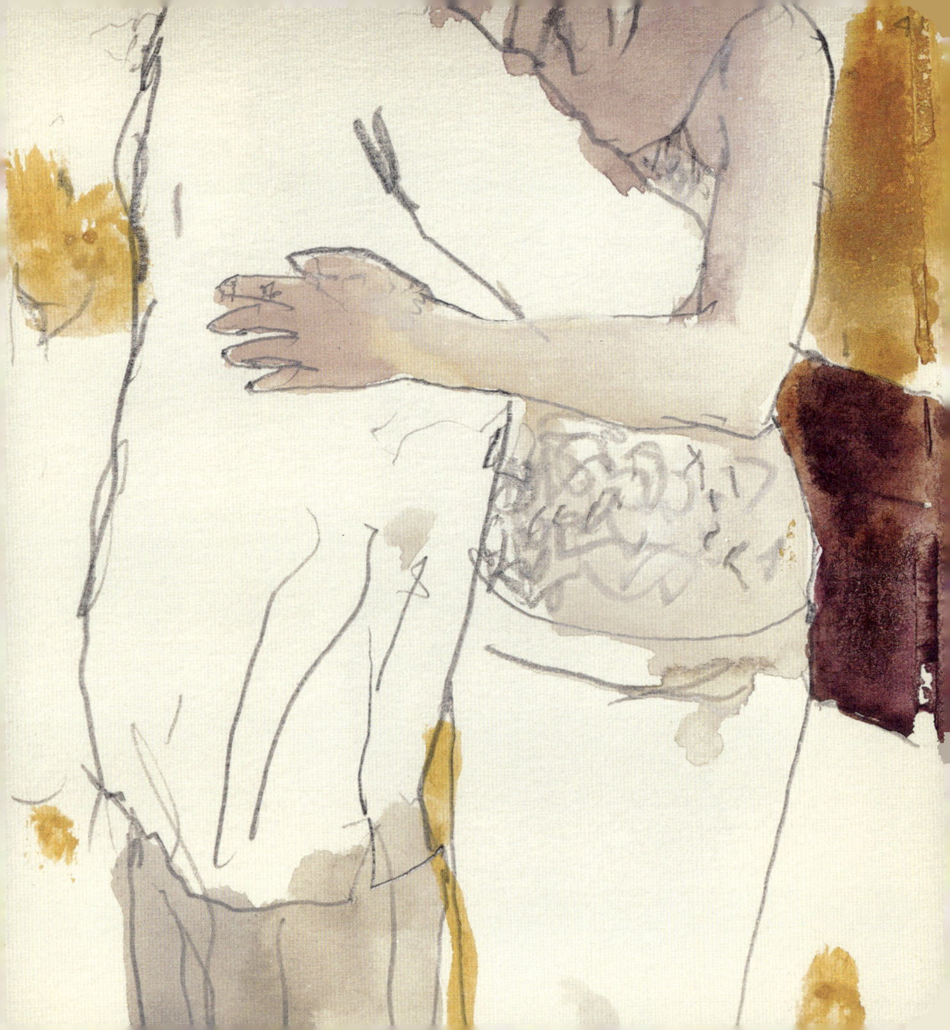

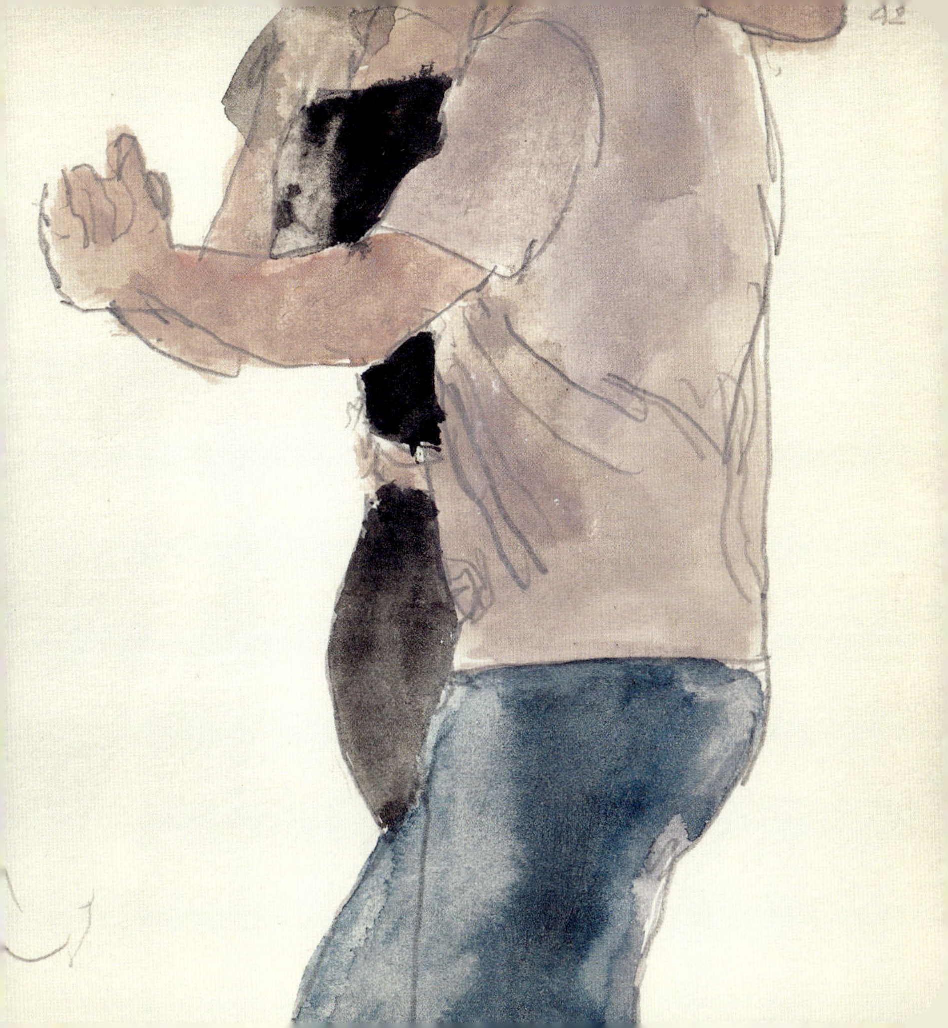

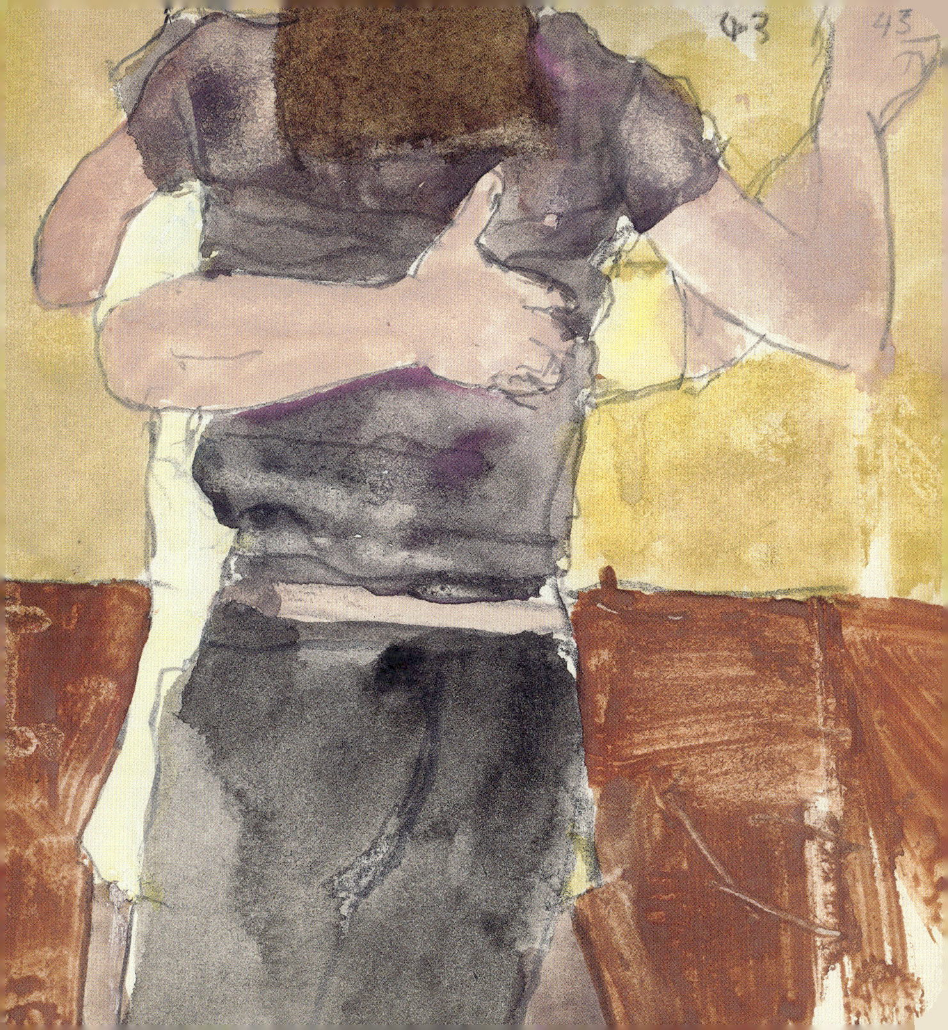
43
43

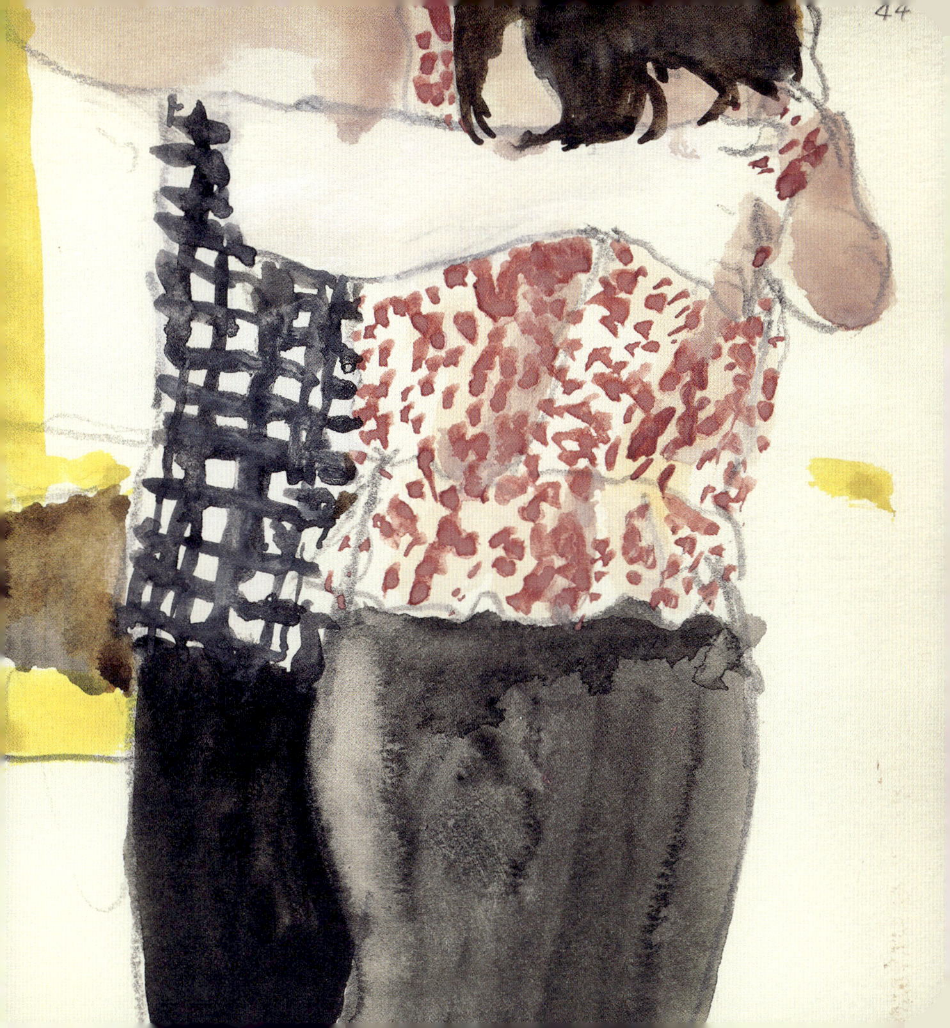
44

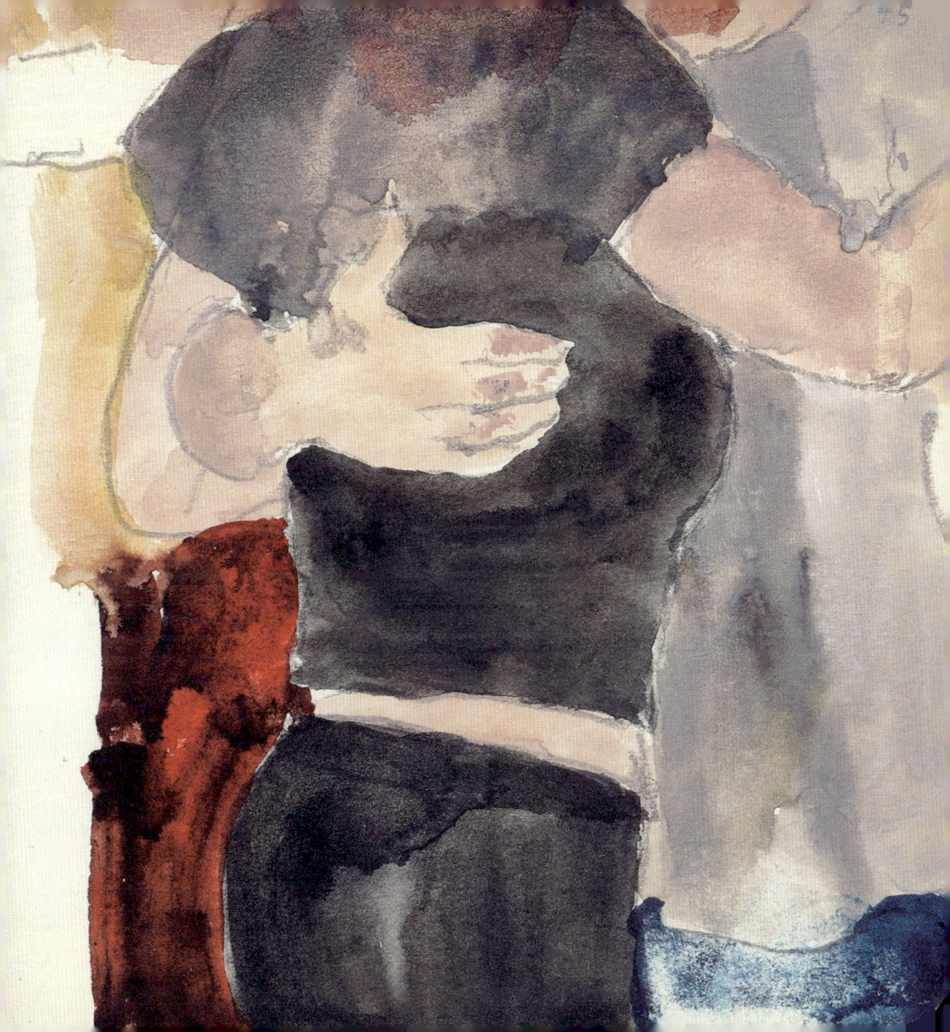

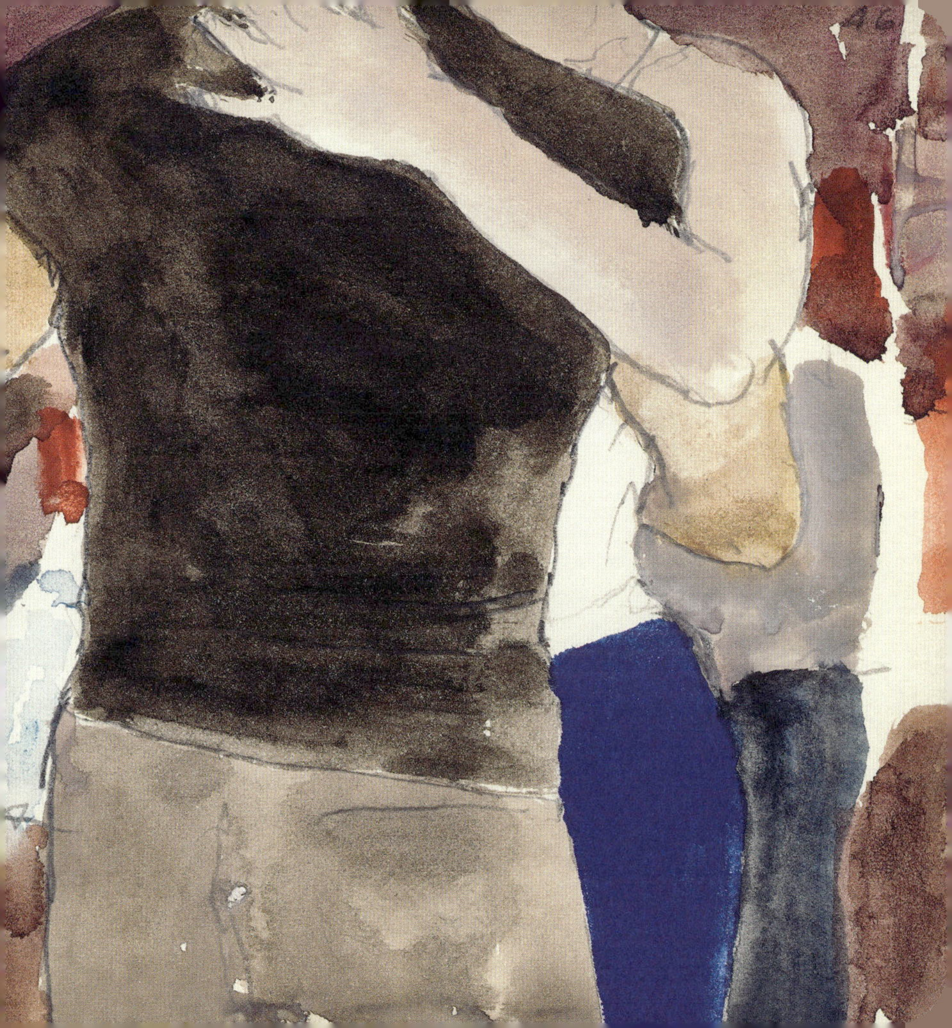

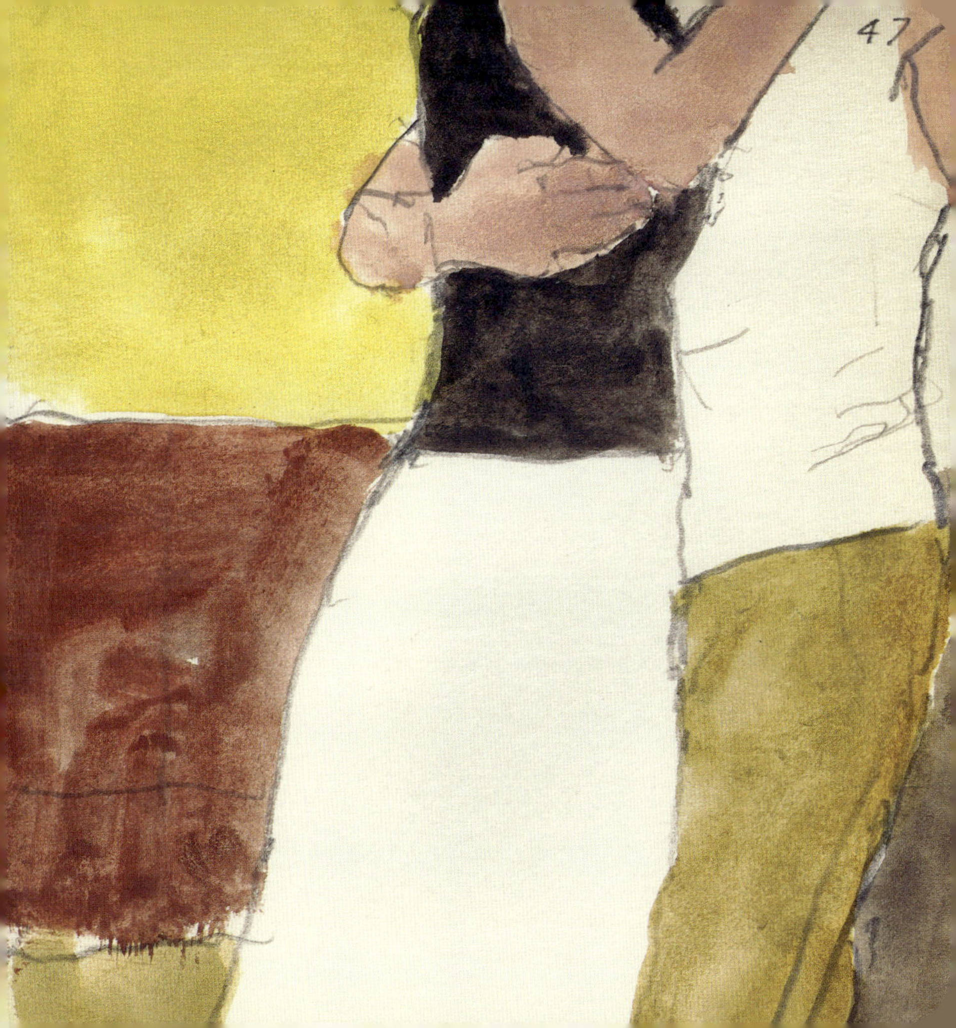
47

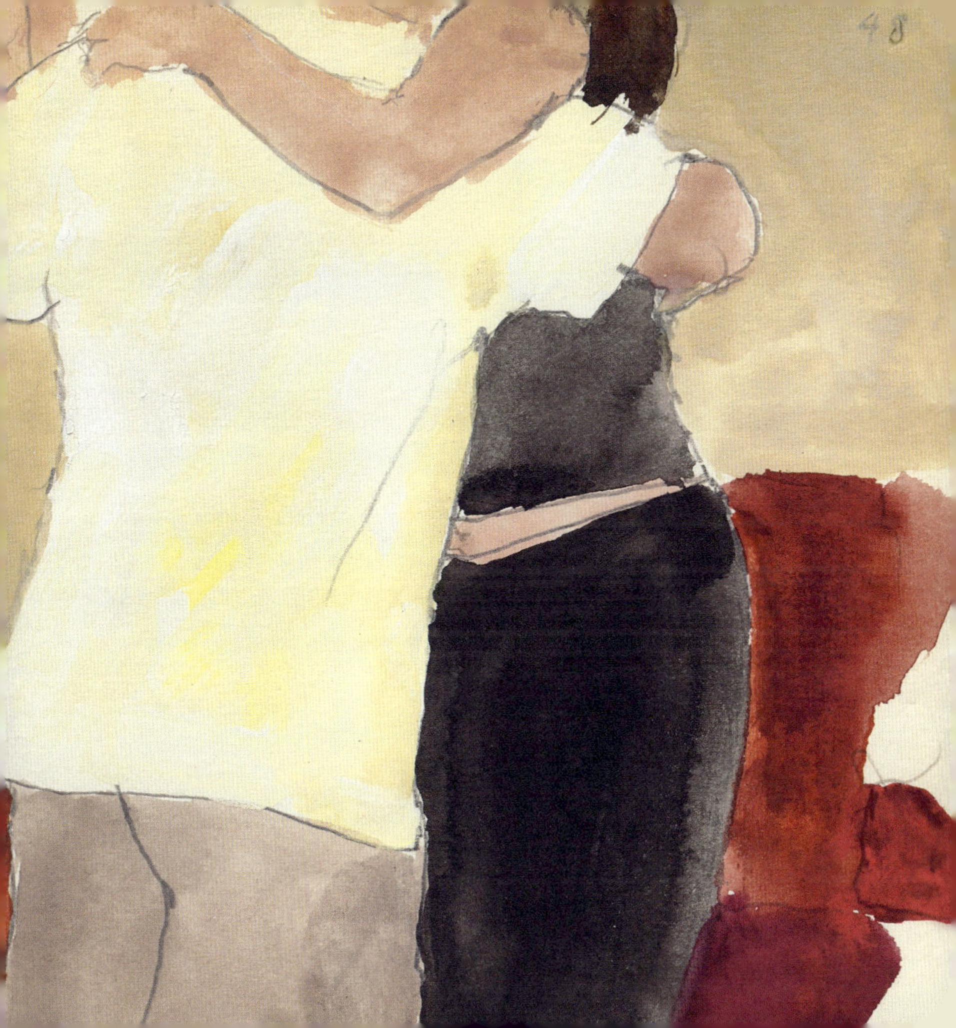
48

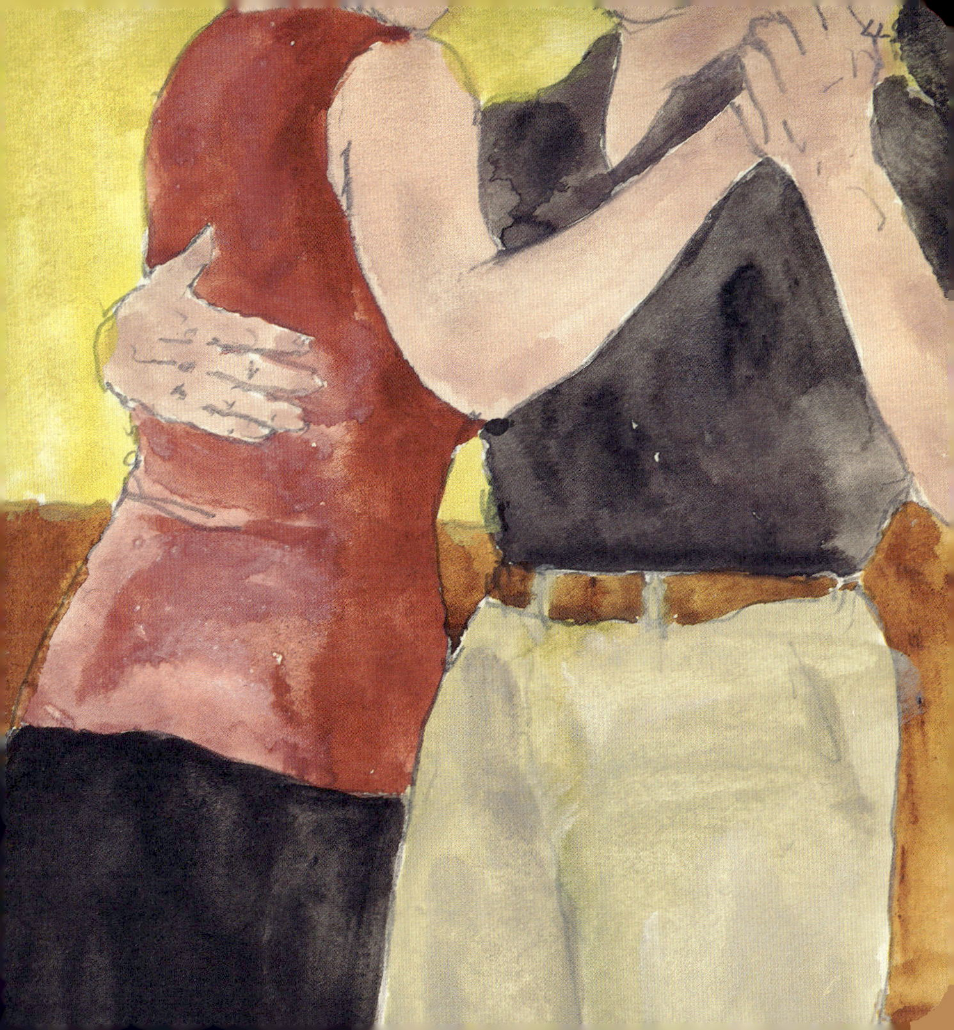

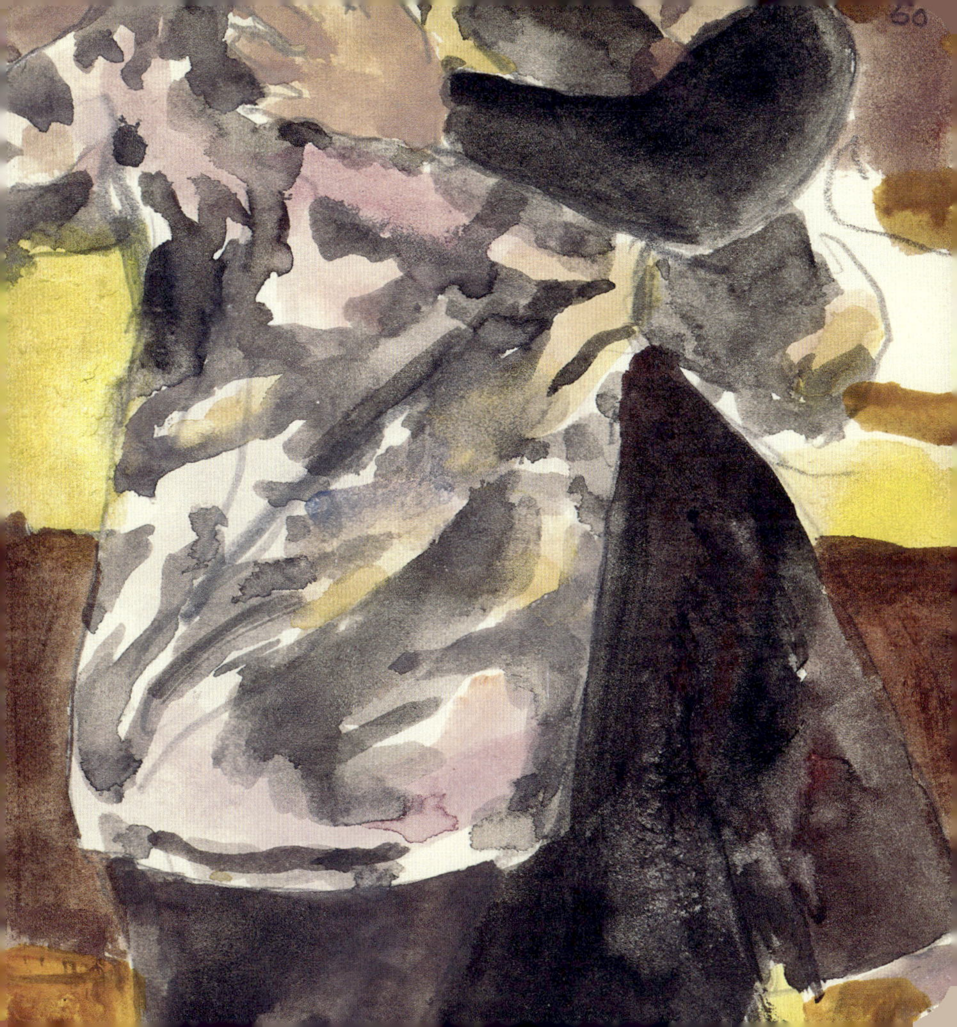
60

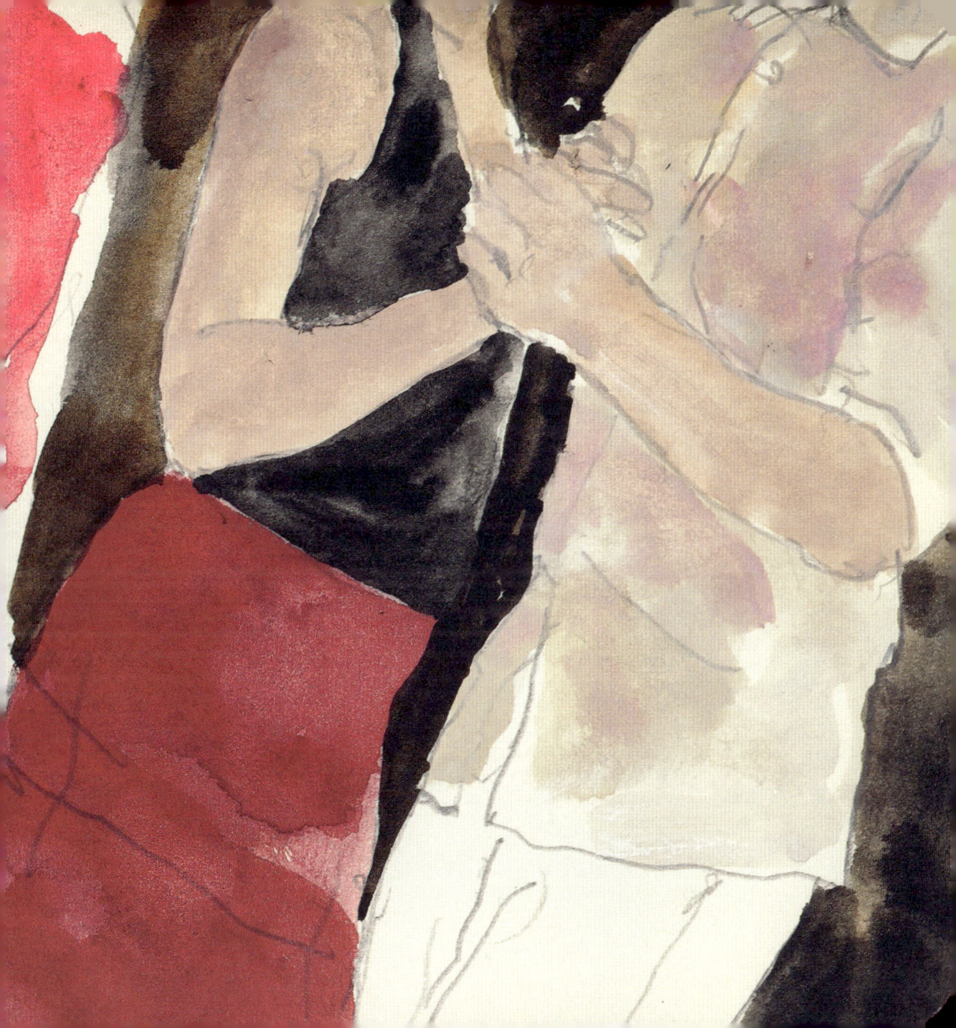

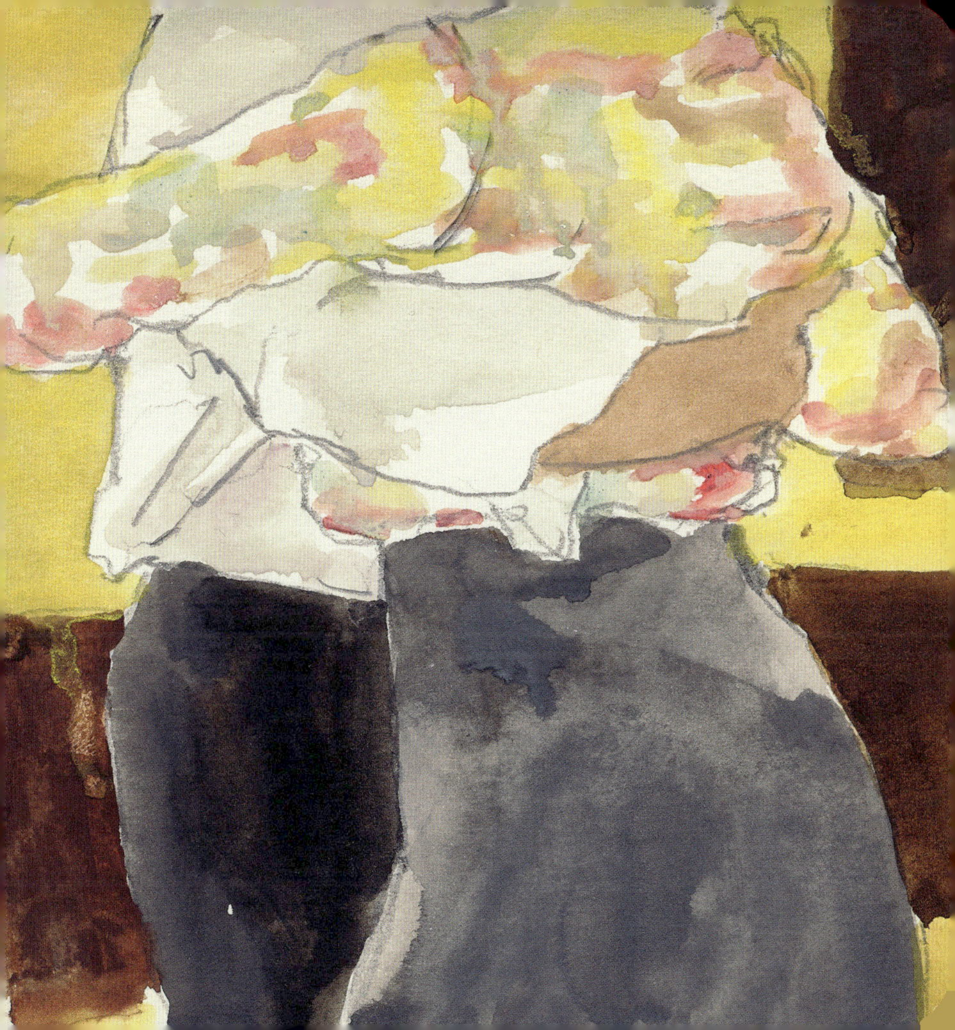

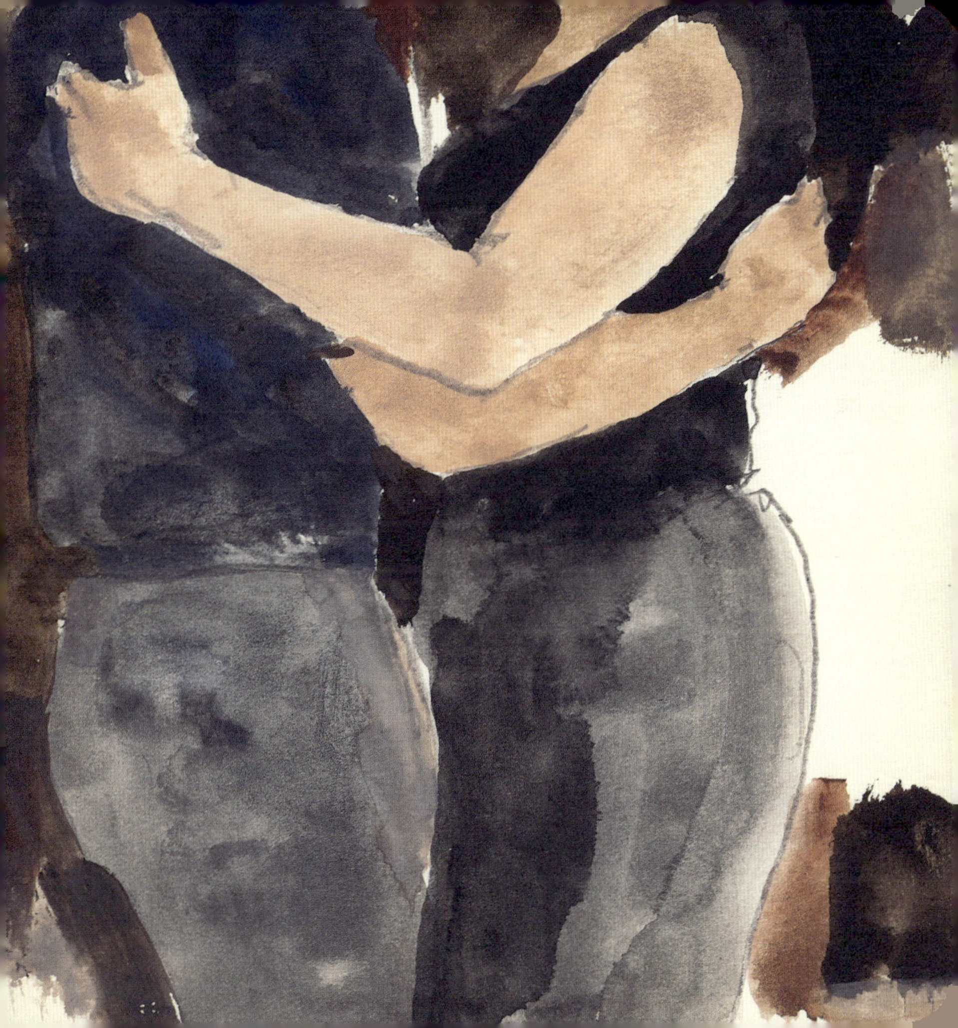

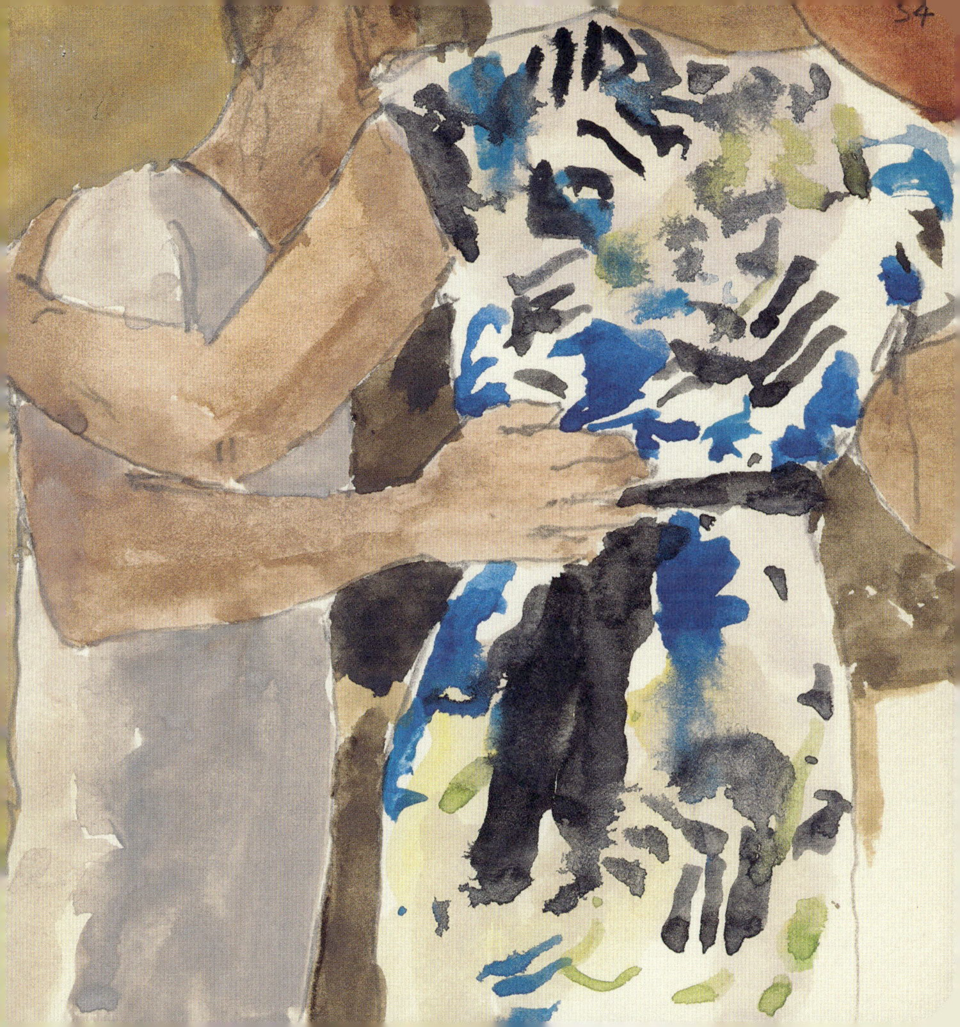
34

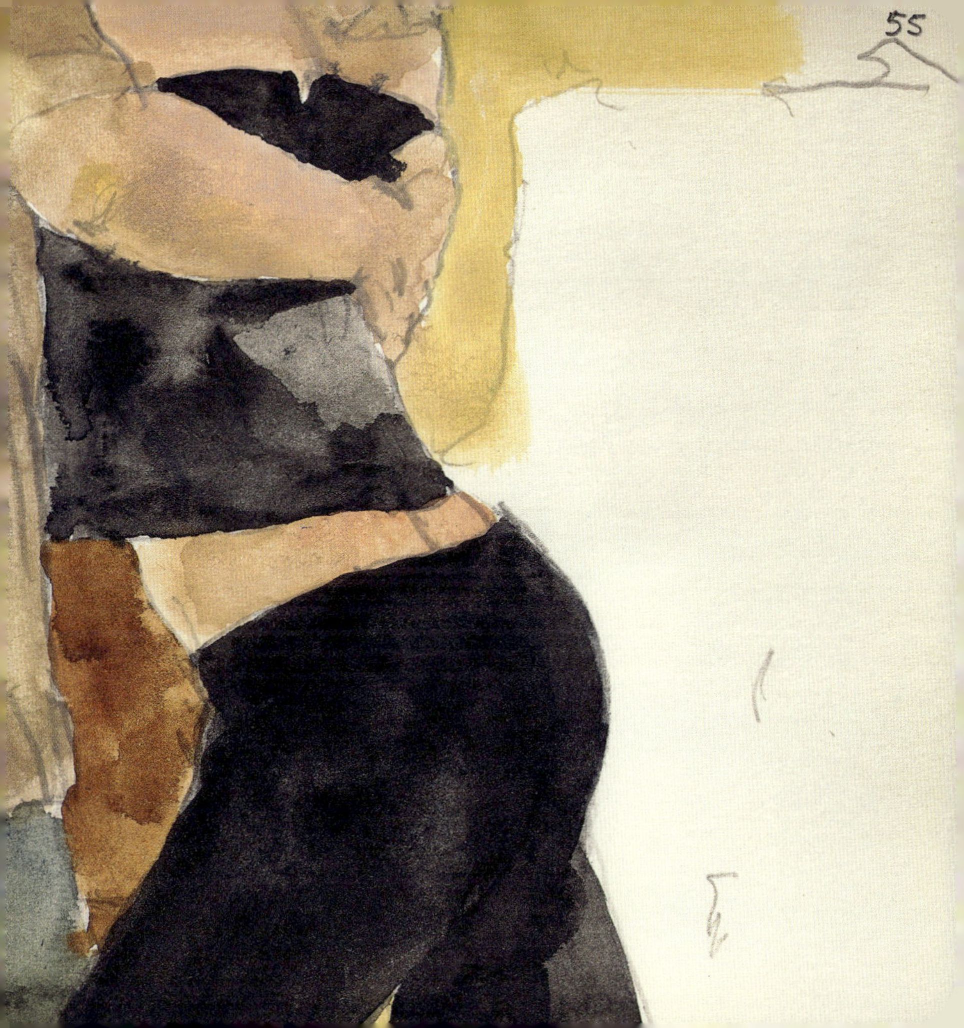
55

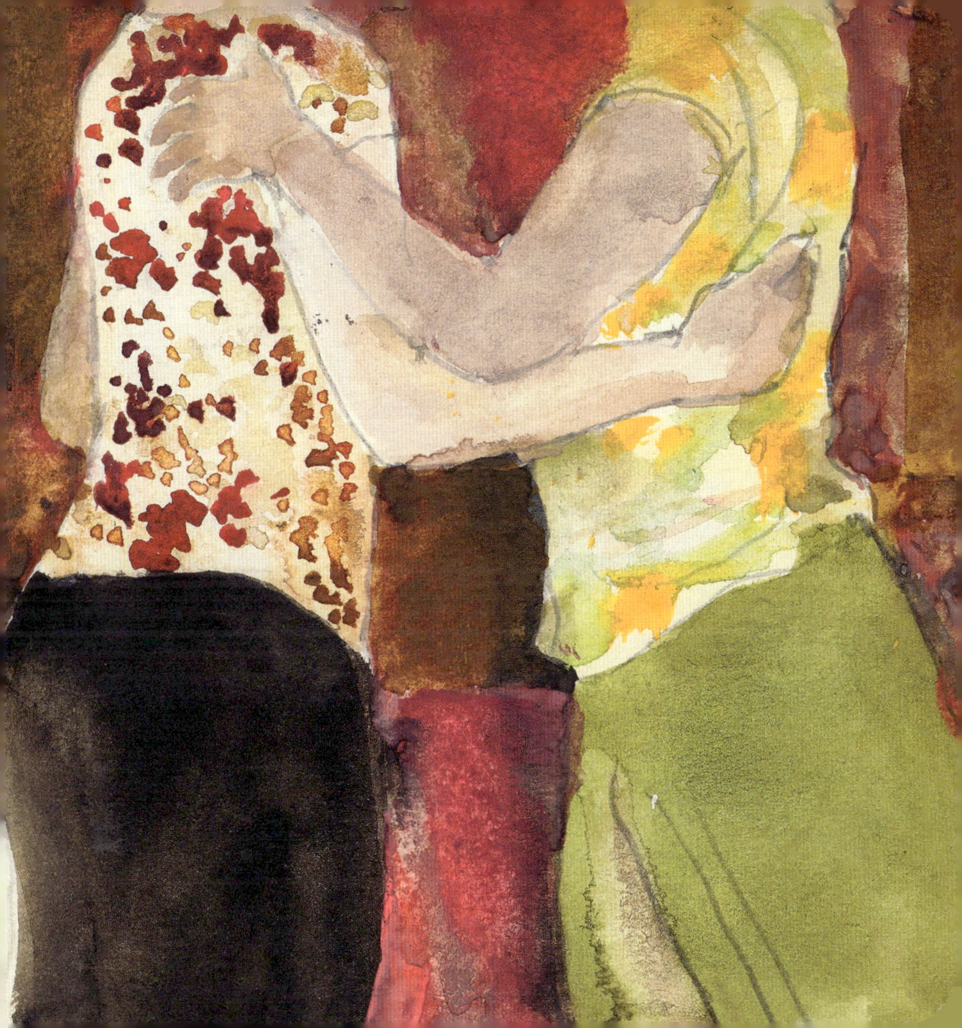

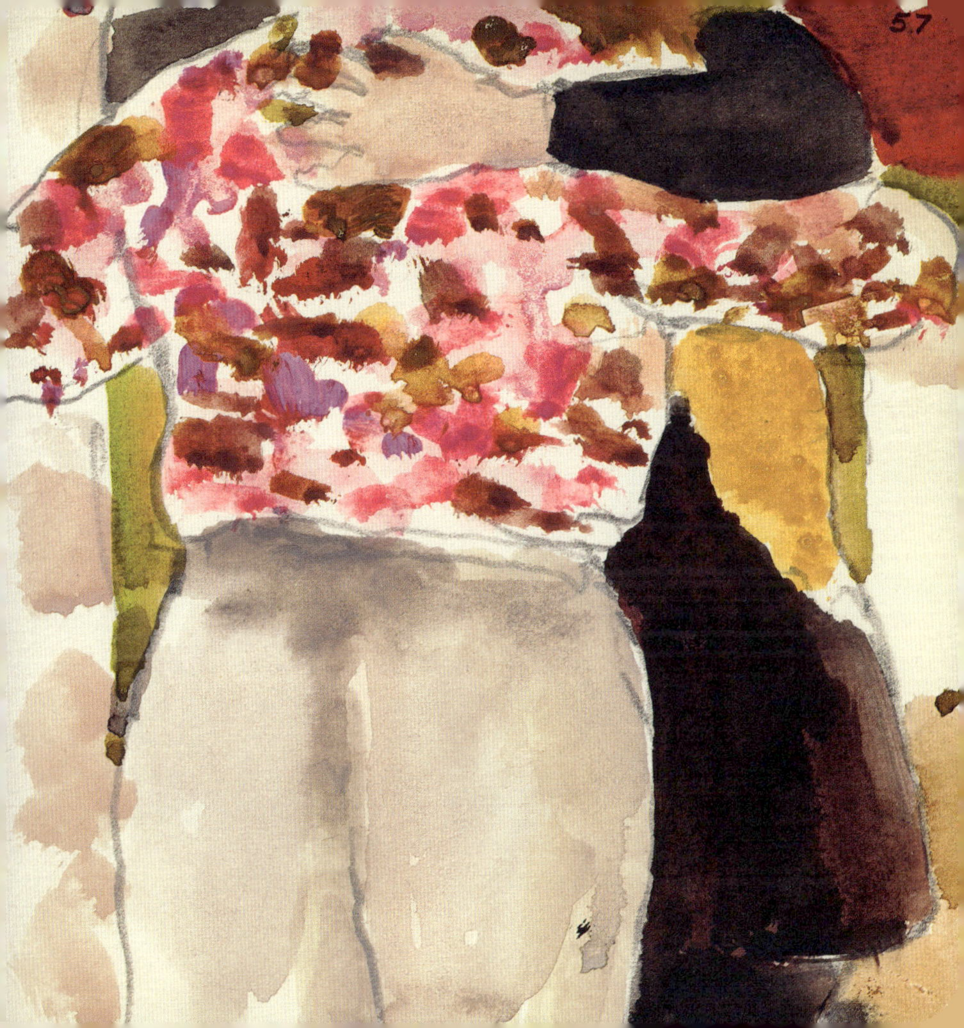
57

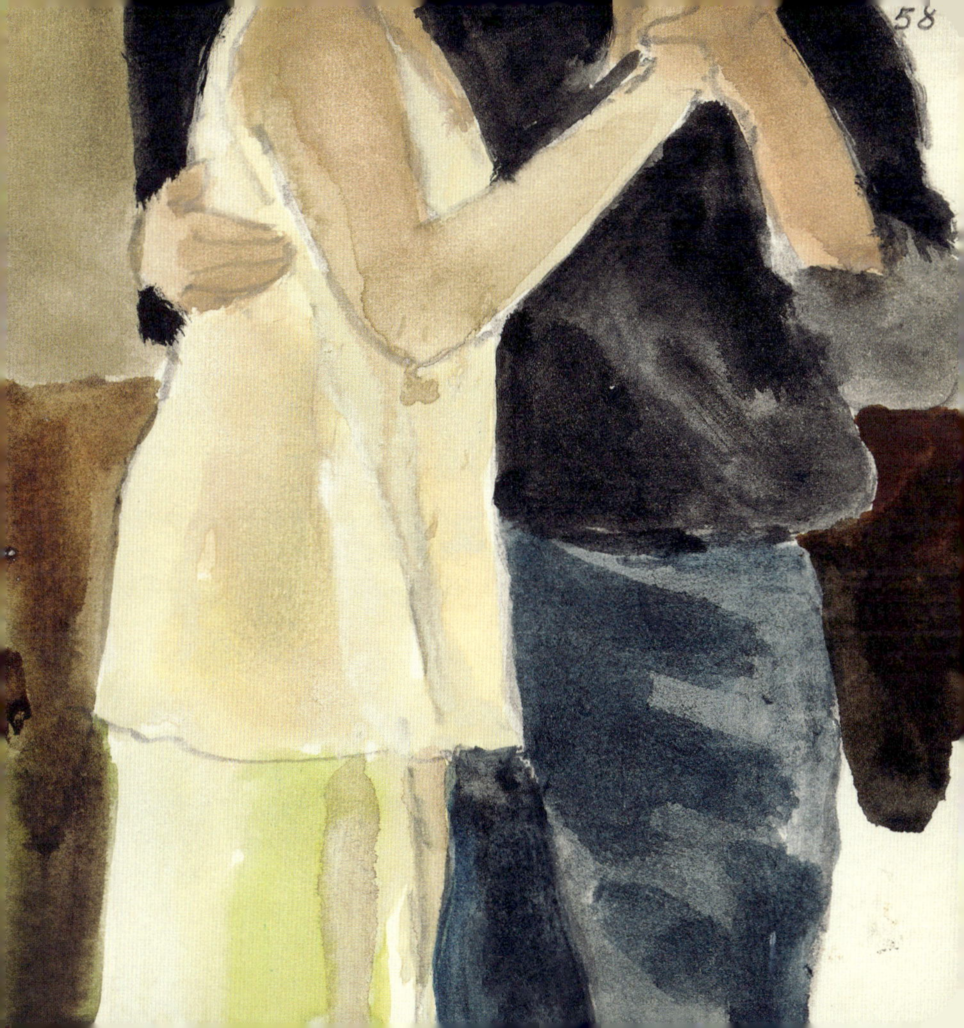

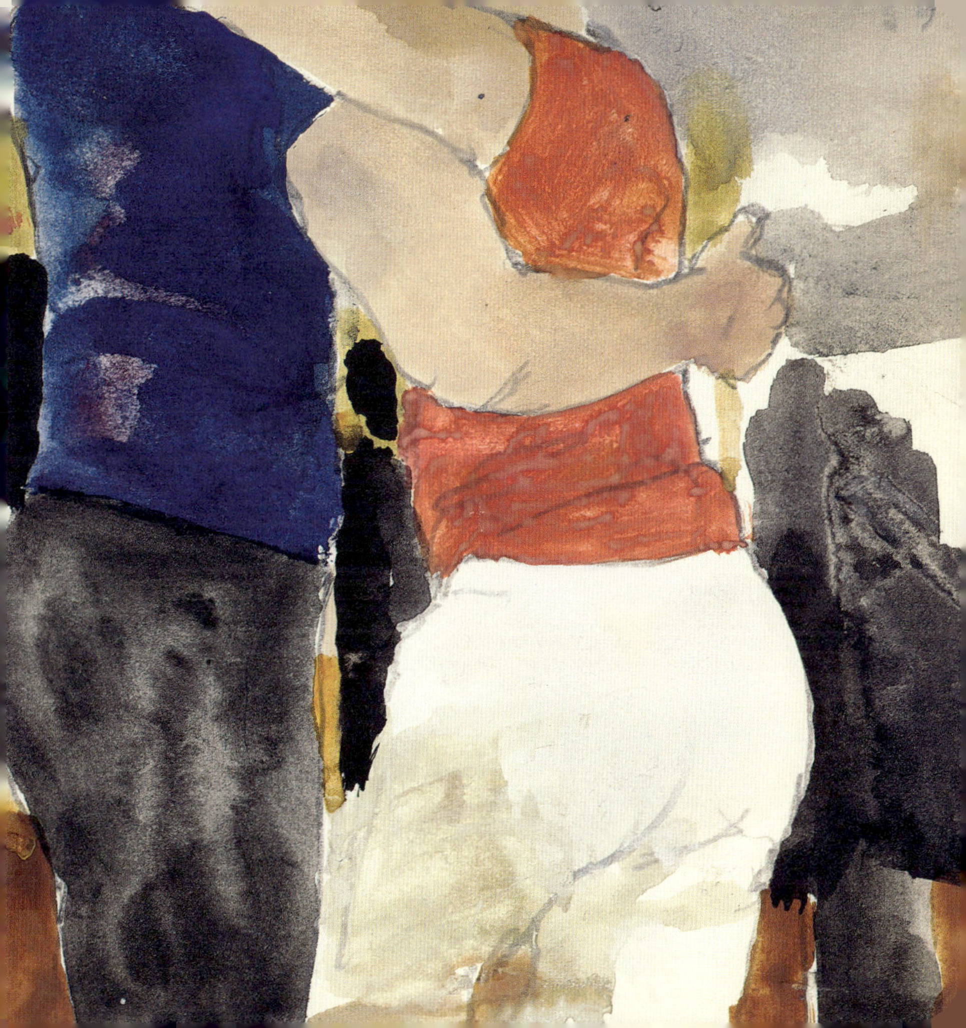

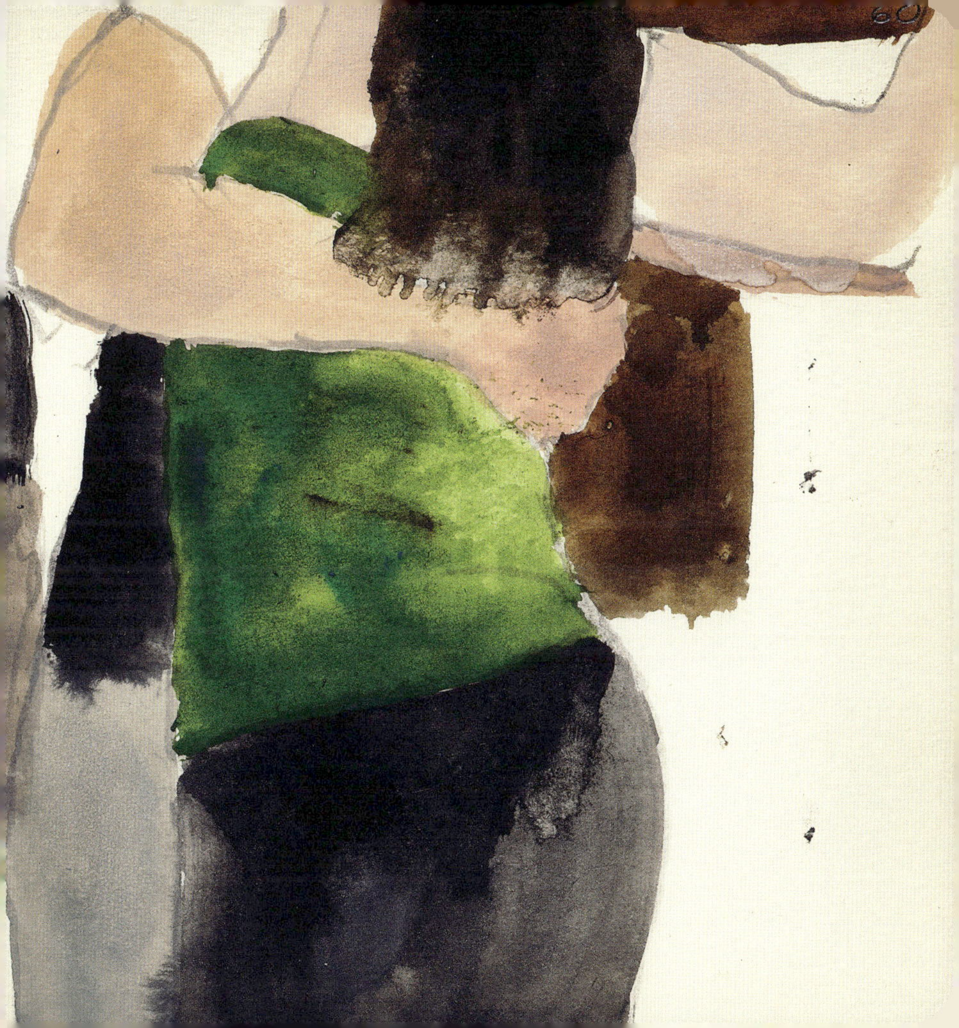
60

British Library Cataloguing-in-Publication Data
A catalogue record for this book is available from the British Library

ISBN 978-1-915815-08-8

Distributed outside the United States and Canada by ACC Art Books Ltd,
Riverside House, Dock Lane, Melton, Woodbridge, IP12 1PE

Distributed in the United States and Canada by ARTBOOK | D.A.P.,
75 Broad Street, Suite 630, New York, NY 10004

Royal Academy Publications
Florence Dassonville, Production and Distribution Co-ordinator
Carola Krueger, Production and Distribution Manager
Peter Sawbridge, Head of Publishing and Editorial Director

Concept: Caroline Hansberry
Design: Maggi Smith
Photography: Prudence Cuming Associates
Printed in Italy by Graphicom